Charles

–

Most Powerful
Revivals

Edited and Updated
By Andrew Strom

Revival School

Charles Finney – Most Powerful Revivals
Copyright © 2004-2008 by Andrew Strom. All rights reserved.

First printing, 2004
Second printing, 2008

Published by: Revival School
www.revivalschool.com
prophetic@revivalschool.com

Wholesale distribution through Lightning Source, Inc.

ISBN-13: 978-0-9799073-6-4

ISBN-10: 0-9799073-6-5

1. Prophets -- History   2. Revival

CONTENTS

*"Revival comes from heaven when heroic
souls enter the conflict determined
to win or die – or if need be, to win and die!
'The kingdom of heaven suffers
violence, and the violent take it by force.'"*
-CHARLES FINNEY

Chapter One

THE EARLY YEARS

It is true that my name has been linked with an extensive movement of revivals, but I approach the subject with reluctance for many reasons. I have kept no diary, and so I must depend on my memory. Having said that, I have been reminded of these revivals so many times, and have so often referred to them in all the years of my ministry, that I am confident that I remember them pretty much as they occurred.

I was born in Warren, Connecticut on August 29, 1792. When I was about two years old, my father moved to Oneida County, New York, which was a wilderness at that time. No Christian meetings were held there. Very few Christian books were to be found. The new settlers, mostly from New England, almost immediately established common schools; but they heard very little intelligent preaching of the Gospel. I went to a common school until I was fifteen or sixteen years old.

Neither of my parents were religious, and among our neighbors there were very few religious people. I seldom heard a sermon, unless it was an occasional one from some traveling minister, or the miserable holding forth of some ignorant preacher who would sometimes be found in that region. The ignorance of these preachers was such that the people would often return from the meetings and spend a considerable time in irrepressible laughter at the strange mistakes which had been made and the absurd things we had been told.

In our neighborhood we had just built a meeting house and brought a pastor in, when my father moved again – to the wilderness skirting the southern shore of Lake Ontario. Here again I lived for several years with no more exposure to Christianity than I had experienced in Oneida County.

When I was about twenty years old I travelled to New Jersey near New York City, where I worked as a teacher. I taught and studied as best I could, and returned to New England twice to attend high school. I considered going to Yale College. My tutor was a graduate of Yale, but he advised me not to go. He said it would be a waste of time, as I could easily accomplish their whole curriculum in two years, while it would cost me four years to graduate from Yale itself. As a result I failed to pursue my school education any further at that time. However, I later acquired some knowledge of Latin, Greek, and Hebrew. But I was never a classical scholar.

My tutor wanted me to join him in running an academy in one of the Southern States. I was inclined to accept his offer, but when I informed my parents, whom I had not seen for four years, they both immediately came after me and convinced me to go home with them to Jefferson county, New York. Thus I became a student in the law office of Squire W in Adams, Jefferson County. This was in 1818.

Up to this time I had never enjoyed what might be called Christian privileges. I had never lived in a praying community, except when I was attending high school in New England; and the Christianity there was not designed to get my attention at all. The preaching was by an old clergyman – an excellent man, truly loved by his people. But he read his sermons in a way that left no impression on my mind at all. He had a monotonous, humdrum way of reading what he had probably written many years before.

To give some idea of his preaching, his written sermons were just large enough to put into a small Bible. I sat in the gallery and saw that he placed his fingers in the Bible at the passages to be quoted during the reading of his sermon. This made it necessary to hold his Bible in both hands. As he proceeded he would liberate one finger after another until the fingers of both hands were read out of their places. When his fingers were all read out, he was near the end of his sermon. His reading was totally monotonous and though the people listened attentively, I have to say it did not seem much like preaching to me.

I often heard people speak well of his sermons, and sometimes they would wonder if he was alluding to things that were happening amongst them. They always seemed curious to know what he was aiming at, especially if there was anything more in his sermon than a dry discussion of doctrine. And this was really quite as good preaching as I had ever listened to anywhere. But anyone can judge whether such preaching was calculated to instruct or interest a young man who neither knew nor cared anything about Christianity.

When I was teaching school in New Jersey, the preaching in the neighborhood was mainly in German. I do not think I heard half a dozen sermons in English during my whole stay in New Jersey, which was about three years.

Thus when I went to Adams to study law, I was almost as ignorant of Christianity as a heathen. I had been brought up mostly in the woods.

At Adams, for the first time, I sat under an educated ministry. Rev. George Gale from Princeton, New Jersey, became pastor of the Presbyterian Church in that place soon after I went there. His preaching was of the old school type. It was thoroughly Calvinistic, and whenever he came out with doctrine, which he seldom did, he would preach what has been called hyper-Calvinism. He was, of course, regarded as highly orthodox; but I didn't get much out of his preaching. As I sometimes told him, he seemed to begin in the middle, and to assume many things which I thought needed to be proved. He seemed to take it for granted that his hearers were theologians, and to assume they understood all the great and fundamental doctrines of the Gospel. I must say that I was more perplexed than helped by his preaching.

Until this time I had never lived where I could attend a prayer meeting. But because one was held by the church near our office every week, I went and listened to the prayers quite often.

In studying law, I found the old authors frequently referring to the Mosaic Law as authority for many of the great principles of common law. This aroused my curiosity so much that I went and bought a Bible, the first I had ever owned; and whenever I found a reference by the law authors to the Bible, I turned to the passage and consulted it. This soon led to me taking a new interest in the Bible, and I read and meditated on it much more than I had ever done before. However, much of it I did not understand.

Mr. Gale was in the habit of dropping in at our office frequently, and seemed anxious to know what impression his sermons had made on me. I used to discuss things frankly with him, and now I think that I sometimes criticized his sermons unmercifully.

I perceived that his own mind could not define what he really meant by a lot of the terminology he used. In fact, I found it impossible to attach any meaning to many of the terms he used all the time. What did he mean by repentance? Was it merely a feeling of sorrow for sin? If it was a change of mind, in what respect was it a change of mind? What did he mean by faith? Was it merely an intellectual state? Was it merely a conviction, or persuasion, that the things stated in the Gospel were true? I could not tell, nor did he seem to truly know himself.

We had many interesting discussions, but they seemed to make me question more and more, rather than satisfying me as to the truth.

But as I read my Bible and attended the prayer meetings, heard Mr. Gale preach, and spoke with him and others, I became very restless. I became convinced that I was in no state to go to heaven if I died. It seemed to me that there must be something in religion that was of infinite importance; and I decided that if the soul was immortal I needed a great change inside me to make it into heaven. But still my mind was not made up as to whether Christianity was true or not. However, the question was too important to leave alone.

I was particularly struck with the fact that the prayers I had listened to from week to week were not being answered, that I could see. When I read my Bible I learned what Christ had said about prayer, and answers to prayer: "Ask and you shall receive, seek and you shall find, knock and it shall be opened unto you." I also read what Christ said – that God is more willing to give His Holy Spirit to them that ask Him, than earthly parents are to give good gifts to their children. I heard them pray continually for the outpouring of the Holy Spirit, and then confess that they did not receive what they asked for.

They urged each other to wake up and pray earnestly for revival, saying that if they did their duty and prayed for the outpouring of the Spirit then revival would come. But in their prayer meetings they would continually confess that they were making no progress towards revival.

This inconsistency, the fact that they prayed so much and were not answered, was a sad stumbling block to me. I didn't know what to make of it. Were these people not truly Christians, and therefore they did not prevail with God; or did I misunderstand the promises and teachings of the Bible, or was I to conclude that the Bible was not true? It was truly bewildering to me, and for awhile it seemed as though it would almost drive me into unbelief. It seemed like the teachings of the Bible did not line up with the facts that were before my eyes.

One time, when I was in one of the prayer meetings, I was asked if I wanted them to pray for me. I told them 'No,' because I did not see that God answered their prayers. I said, "I suppose I need to be prayed for, because I am conscious that I am a sinner; but I do not see that it will do any good for you to pray for me. You are continually asking, but you do not receive. You have been praying for a revival ever since I have been in Adams, and yet you do not have one. You have prayed enough since I have attended these meetings to have prayed the devil out of Adams, if there is any virtue in your prayers. But here you are praying on, and complaining still." I was quite irritable, I think, because at the time I was continually being brought face to face with spiritual truth – which was a new thing for me.

But on further reading of my Bible, it struck me that the reason why their prayers were not answered was because they did not meet God's conditions for answered prayer. They did not pray in faith, expecting God to give them what they asked for.

For some time this thought sat in my mind as a confused question rather than a definite answer. But it gave me a sense of relief in regard to the truth of the Gospel; and after struggling for two or three years, my mind became quite settled that whatever questions there might be, either in my own or my pastor's mind, the Bible was the true Word of God.

Having settled this fact, I was brought face to face with the question of whether I would accept Christ as presented in the Gospel, or pursue a worldly course of life. The Holy Spirit was working on me so strongly that I could not leave this question alone for long.

Chapter Two

CONVERSION

On a Sunday evening in autumn 1821, I made up my mind that I would settle the question of my soul's salvation at once – that if possible I would make my peace with God. But because I was very busy in the office, I knew that unless I was really determined, I would never do it. So I decided, as much as possible, to avoid all business and other distractions, and focus entirely on the salvation of my soul. I carried this out as best I could. I was required to be in the office quite a lot, but I was not too busy on Monday or Tuesday, and had the opportunity to read my Bible and pray most of the time.

However, I was very proud without knowing it. I had convinced myself that I didn't care what others thought of me. In fact, I had been quite consistent in attending prayer meetings and going to church while in Adams. The Christians had begun to think that I must be anxious about my salvation. But I found, when I came to face the question, that I was very unwilling for anyone to know that I was seeking the salvation of my soul. When I prayed I would only whisper my prayer, after having stopped up the keyhole in case someone discovered me praying. Up until then I had left my Bible lying on the table with my law books, and it never occurred to me to be ashamed of being found reading it, any more than I would be ashamed of being found reading any of my other books.

But after I had decided to seek salvation, I kept my Bible out of sight. If I was reading it when anybody came in I would throw my law books on top of it, to create the impression that I had not had it in my hand. Instead of being outspoken and willing to talk with anybody and everybody on the subject like before, I found that I didn't want to talk to anyone. I didn't want to see the minister because I did not want him to know how I felt, and anyway I had no confidence that he would understand and give me the direction I needed. I avoided conversation with the elders of the church, or with any of the Christian people. I was ashamed to let them know how I felt on one the hand, and on the other, I was afraid they would misdirect me. I felt myself shut up to the Bible.

During Monday and Tuesday my convictions increased, but still it seemed as if my heart grew harder. I could not shed a tear; I could not pray. I had no opportunity to pray above my breath, and I often felt that if I could be alone where I could use my voice and let it out, then I would find relief in prayer. I was shy and avoided speaking to anybody on any subject. I tried to do this in a way that would cause no-one to suspect that I was seeking the salvation of my soul.

Tuesday night I had become very nervous; and in the night a strange feeling came over me as if I was about to die. I knew that if I did I would sink down to hell; but I quieted myself as best I could until morning.

At an early hour I started for the office. But just before I arrived, something seemed to confront me with questions like these: "What are you waiting for? Didn't you promise to give your heart to God? What are you trying to do? Are you trying to work out a righteousness of your own?"

Just at this point the whole question of Gospel salvation opened up to me in a wonderful way. I think I saw, as clearly as I ever have in my life, the reality and fullness of the atonement of Christ. I saw that His work was a finished work; and that instead of having, or needing, any righteousness of my own to recommend me to God, I had to submerge myself in the righteousness of Christ. Gospel salvation seemed to be an offer of something to be accepted; and that it was full and complete; and that all that was necessary on my part was to get my own consent to give up my sins and accept Christ. Instead of being something I could achieve by working myself, salvation was a thing to be found entirely in the Lord Jesus

Christ, who presented Himself before me as my God and my Savior.

Without being aware of it, I had stopped in the street right where the inward voice seemed to arrest me. How long I remained there I cannot say. But after this revelation, the next question seemed to be: "Will you accept it now, today?" I replied," Yes, I will accept it today, or I will die in the attempt."

North of the village, over a hill, lay some woods where I went walking most days when the weather was fine. It was now October, and the time was past for my frequent walks there. But now, instead of going to the office, I turned and started for the woods, feeling that I must be alone and away from all human eyes, so that I could pour out my prayer to God.

But still my pride made itself felt. As I went over the hill, it occurred to me that someone might see me and suspect that I was going away to pray. Yet probably there was not a person on earth that would have thought such a thing. But my pride and fear of man was so great that I skulked along under the fence until I got so far out of sight that no one from the village could see me. I then veered into the woods about a quarter of a mile and found a place where some large trees had fallen across each other, leaving an open space between. I ducked in there and knelt down to pray. As I had turned to go up into the woods, I remember saying, "I will give my heart to God, or I never will come down from there." I repeated this on the way up: "I will give my heart to God before I ever come down again."

But when I attempted to pray I found that my heart would not pray. I had assumed that if I could only find a place where I could speak aloud, without being overheard, I could pray freely. But when I came to try, I was dumb; that is, I had nothing to say to God. I could only say a few words, and those without heart. In attempting to pray I would hear a rustling in the leaves, and would stop and look up to see if somebody was coming. I did this several times.

Finally I found myself verging on despair. I said to myself, "I cannot pray. My heart is dead to God and will not pray." I was kicking myself for having promised to give my heart to God before I left the woods. When I came to try, I found I could not give my heart to God. My inward soul hung back, and there was no going out of my heart to God. I began to feel that it was too late; that God must have given me up and I was past hope.

I could not believe how rash I had been, to promise that I would give my heart to God that day or die in the attempt. It seemed like it was binding on my soul; and yet I was going to break my vow. A terrible weight of discouragement came over me, and I felt almost too weak to stand upon my knees.

Just at this moment I again thought I heard someone approach me, and I opened my eyes to see. But right there the revelation of my pride, as the great difficulty that stood in the way, was clearly shown to me. An overwhelming sense of my sinfulness in being ashamed to have someone see me on my knees before God, took hold of me. I cried out at the top of my voice that I would not leave that place if all the men on earth and all the devils in hell surrounded me. "What!" I said, "such a degraded sinner as me, on my knees confessing my sins to a holy God; and ashamed to have any human being find me on my knees before Him!" The sin appeared awful, infinite. It broke me down before the Lord.

Just at that point this passage of Scripture seemed to drop into my mind with a flood of light: "You will seek me and find me, when you search for me with all your heart." I instantly seized hold of this. I had intellectually believed the Bible before; but never had I seen the truth that faith was a willing trust instead of an intellectual state. I was suddenly conscious of trusting at that moment in God's trustworthiness. Somehow I knew that that was a passage of Scripture, though I do not think I had ever read it. I knew that it was God's word, and God's voice, as it were, that spoke to me. I cried to Him, "Lord, I take you at your word. You know that I am searching for you with all my heart, and that I have come here to pray to you; and you have promised to hear me."

That seemed to settle the question that I could perform my vow that very day. The Spirit seemed to emphasise the phrase, "When you search for me with all your heart." I told the Lord that I would take Him at his word; that He could not lie; and that therefore I was sure that He heard my prayer, and would allow me to find Him.

He then gave me many other promises from the Old and New Testaments, including some powerful promises regarding our Lord Jesus Christ. I never can, in words, make any human understand how precious and true those promises appeared to me. I took them one after the other as infallible truth, the assertions of God who could not lie. They did not seem to fall so much into my intellect as into my heart, and I seized hold of them with the grasp of a drowning man.

I continued to pray this way, and to receive promises for a long time. I prayed until my mind became so full that, before I was aware of it, I was on my feet and tripping up the hill towards the road. The question of becoming converted had not even arisen in my thoughts; but as I went up, brushing through the leaves and bushes, I recall saying with emphasis, "If I am ever converted, I will preach the Gospel."

I soon reached the road that led to the village, and began to think about what had just happened; and I found that my mind had become wonderfully quiet and peaceful. I said to myself, "What is this? I must have grieved the Holy Spirit entirely away. I have lost all my conviction. I don't have one bit of concern about my soul; The Spirit must have left me." It seemed like I had never been so unconcerned about my own salvation in my life.

Then I remembered what I had said to God while I was on my knees – that I would take Him at his word. In fact I remembered a whole lot of things that I had said, and concluded that it was no wonder the Spirit had left me. For such a sinner to take hold of God's Word in that way must surely be presumption if not blasphemy. I concluded that in my excitement I had grieved the Holy Spirit, and perhaps committed the unpardonable sin.

I walked quietly towards the village, and my mind was so perfectly quiet that it seemed as if all nature listened. It was the 10th of October, and a very pleasant day. I had gone into the woods immediately after an early breakfast and when I returned to the village I found it was dinner time. Yet I had been completely unaware of the time that had passed. It seemed like I had been gone from the village for only a short time.

But how could I account for the quiet of my mind? I tried to recall my convictions, to get back the load of sin which had been weighing me down. But all sense of sin, all consciousness of sin or guilt, had departed from me. I said to myself, "What is this, that I cannot arouse any sense of guilt in my soul – a sinner like me?" I tried in vain to make myself anxious. I was so quiet and peaceful that I tried to feel concerned about that, in case it was the result of having grieved the Spirit away. But try as I might, I could not make myself anxious at all. The calm in my mind was breathtaking. It can't be described in words. The thought of God was sweet to my mind, and the most profound spiritual tranquility had taken me over.

I went to dinner, and found I had no appetite to eat. Then I went to the office, and found that Squire W had gone to dinner. I took down my bass viol as I often did, and began to play and sing some spiritual songs. But as soon as I started to sing those holy words, I began to weep. It seemed as if my heart was all liquid, and my feelings were in such a state that I could not hear my own voice singing without causing my emotions to overflow. I tried to keep back the tears, but couldn't. So I put my instrument away and stopped singing.

After dinner we were busy moving our books and furniture to another office. Because we were so busy, we hardly spoke much all afternoon. But my mind remained in that profoundly tranquil state. Everything appeared to be going right, and nothing seemed to ruffle or disturb me in the least.

Late that afternoon I began to feel compelled that as soon as I was left alone in the new office, I would try to pray again. I was not going to abandon the subject of Christianity and give it up. Though I no longer had any concern about my soul, I would still continue to pray.

As darkness fell, Squire W said goodnight and went home. I had accompanied him to the door, and as I closed the door and turned around, my heart seemed to be liquid within me. All my feelings seemed to rise and flow out, and the cry of my heart was, "I want to pour my whole soul out to God." The intensity was so great that I rushed into the room behind the front office, to pray.

There was no fire and no light in the room, but it appeared to me as if it was perfectly light. As I went in and shut the door, it seemed like I met the Lord Jesus Christ face to face. It seemed to me that I saw Him as I would see any other man. He said nothing, but looked at me in a way that broke me right down at his feet. I poured out my soul to Him. I wept aloud like a child, and made whatever confessions I could. It seemed to me that I bathed His feet with my tears; and yet I had no distinct impression that I touched Him.

I must have continued this way for quite some time, but I was too absorbed to remember anything I said. I know that as soon as my mind became calm enough, I returned to the front office, and found that the fire was nearly burned out. But as I turned and was about to take a seat by the fire, I received a mighty baptism of the Holy Spirit. Without any expectation of it, without any thought in my mind that there was any such thing for me, the Holy Spirit descended upon me in a way that seemed to go through me, body and soul. It was like a wave of electricity, going through and through me. Indeed it seemed to come in waves and waves of liquid love. It seemed like the very breath of God. I remember distinctly that it seemed to fan me, like immense wings.

No words can express the wonderful love that filled my heart. I wept aloud with joy and love; I literally bellowed out the inexpressible floods of my heart. These waves came over me and over me, one after the other, until I cried out, "I will die if these waves continue." I said, "Lord, I cannot bear any more." Yet I had no fear of death.

How long I continued in this state, with this baptism continuing to roll over me and go through me, I do not know. But I know it was late in the evening when a member of my choir – for I was the leader of the choir – came into the office to see me. He found me in this state of loud weeping, and said to me, "Mr. Finney, what's wrong?" I could not answer for some time. He then said, "Are you in pain?" I gathered myself up as best I could, and replied, "No, but so happy that I cannot live."

He turned and left the office, and in a few minutes returned with one of the elders of the church, whose shop was nearby. This elder was a very serious man, and I had scarcely ever seen him laugh. When he came in I was in much the same state as when the young man went out to call him. He asked me how I felt and I began to tell him. Instead of saying anything, he fell into the most spasmodic laughter. It seemed as if it was impossible for him to keep from laughing from the very bottom of his heart.

There was a young man in the neighborhood who was a close friend. I learned later that our minister had repeatedly talked with him about Christianity, and warned him against being misled by me. He told him that I was very dismissive of the faith, and he thought that if he associated with me he would be led astray.

After we were both converted, my friend told me that he had said to Mr. Gale several times that my conversations had often impacted him more, spiritually, than his preaching. I had shared a lot of my inner thoughts with this young man.

But just when I was describing my feelings to the elder, this young man came into the office. I was sitting with my back to the door and barely noticed that he came in. He listened with amazement to what I was saying, and the first I knew he partly fell on the floor and cried out in the greatest agony, "Please pray for me!" The elder of the church and the other man knelt down and began to pray for him, and when they had prayed, I prayed for him myself. Soon afterwards they all went home and left me alone.

The question then arose in my mind, "Why did the elder laugh like that? Did he think that I was under a delusion, or mad?" This suggestion brought a kind of darkness over my mind and I began to ask myself whether it was proper for such a sinner as I had been to pray for that young man. A cloud seemed to come over me and not long afterwards I went to bed, not distressed, but still at a loss to know what to make of things. Even after the baptism I had received, I went to bed without knowing for sure that my peace was made with God.

I soon fell asleep, but woke almost immediately because of the great flow of God's love in my heart. I was so filled with love that I could not sleep. Eventually I fell asleep again, only to be woken in the same way. When I awoke, the dark cloud would return, and the love that seemed to be in my heart would die down; but as soon as I went to sleep, it was so warm within me that I would immediately awake. This continued until late into the night. Finally I obtained some sound sleep.

When I awoke in the morning the sun had risen, and was pouring a clear light into my room. Words cannot express the impression that this sunlight made on me. Instantly the baptism that I had received the night before returned in much the same way. I went onto my knees and wept aloud with joy. For some time I was so overwhelmed with the baptism of the Spirit that I could not do anything but pour out my soul to God. It seemed as if this morning's baptism was accompanied by a gentle rebuke, and the Spirit seemed to say to me, "Will you doubt? Will you doubt?" I cried, "No! I will not doubt, I cannot doubt." He then cleared the subject up in such a way that it was impossible for me to doubt that the Spirit of God had taken possession of my soul.

In this state I was taught about 'justification by faith' as an actual experience. I had never realized that justification was a basic doctrine of the Gospel before. In fact I didn't really know what it meant. But I could now see and understand what was meant by the passage, "Being justified by faith, we have peace with God through our Lord Jesus Christ." I could see that the moment I believed, while up in the woods, all sense of condemnation had entirely dropped out of my mind; and that from that moment I could not feel a sense of guilt or condemnation by any effort that I could make. My sense of guilt was gone, my sins were gone, and I don't think I felt any more sense of guilt than if I never had sinned.

This was just the revelation I needed. I felt myself justified by faith and, as far as I could see, I was in a state in which I did not sin. Instead of feeling that I was sinning all the time, my heart was so full of love that it overflowed. My cup ran over with blessing and love, and I could not feel that I was sinning against God. Nor could I recover the least sense of guilt for my past sins. However, I didn't say anything to anyone about this experience of justification at that time.

Chapter Three

REVIVAL BREAKS OUT

That same morning, the waves of love and salvation were still flowing over me when Squire W came into the office. I said a few words to him about his salvation. He looked at me with surprise, but made no reply. He dropped his head, and after standing a few minutes left the office. I thought no more of it, but learned later that the remark I had made pierced him like a sword and he did not recover until he was converted.

Soon afterwards, Deacon B came into the office and said to me, "Mr. Finney, don't you remember that my case is being tried at ten o'clock this morning? I suppose you are ready?" He had paid me a retainer to act as his attorney in a lawsuit. I replied to him, "Deacon B, I have a retainer from the Lord Jesus Christ to represent His case, and I cannot represent yours." He looked at me with astonishment, and said, "What do you mean?" I told him in a few words that I had enlisted in the cause of Christ, and that he must find somebody else for his lawsuit; I could not do it. He dropped his head and went out, without making any reply. A few moments later through the window, I saw that he was standing in the road, seemingly lost in thought. I later learned that he went and settled his lawsuit, and then gave himself to prayer. He soon got into a much higher spiritual state than he had ever been in before.

I went out to talk with anyone and everyone about their souls. I had the impression that God wanted me to preach the Gospel, and that I must begin immediately. Somehow I seemed to know it. If you ask me how, I cannot tell you. But somehow I knew it with a certainty that was past all doubt.

When I was first convicted, the thought had occurred to me that if I was ever converted I would have to leave my profession, of which I was very fond, and go preaching the Gospel. This stumbled me at first. I felt I had worked too hard and studied too long to think of becoming a Christian, if it meant I would have to become a preacher. But in the end I decided to submit the question to God. And after that I forgot all about it, until it came back to me on my way back from praying in the woods.

But now after receiving these baptisms of the Spirit, I was quite willing to preach the Gospel. In fact I was unwilling to do anything else. I no longer had any desire to practice law. Everything in that direction felt empty, and had no attraction for me at all. I had no desire to make money. I had no hunger for worldly pleasures of any kind. My whole mind was taken up with Jesus and His salvation, and worldly things seemed to be of very little concern. Nothing could compare with the value of souls; and no work could be so sweet, and no employment so vital, as that of presenting Christ to a dying world.

And so out I went to talk with anyone I might meet. First I dropped in at the shop of a shoemaker, who was a man of prayer. I found him talking with a son of one of the elders of the church, and this young man was defending Universalism. The shoemaker turned to me and said, "Mr. Finney, what do you think of the argument of this young man?" He then shared what had been said in defense of Universalism. The answer seemed so obvious to me that in a moment I was able to blow the argument to the wind. The young man saw that his argument was gone, and he simply walked out without saying a word. But I saw that instead of going along the street, he went around the shop, climbed over the fence, and was heading straight across the field toward the woods. I thought no more about it until evening, when the young man reappeared, telling of his conversion. He said he had gone up into the woods and given his heart to God.

I spoke with many people that day, and I believe the Spirit of God made lasting impressions on every one of them. I cannot remember any that I spoke with, who were not converted soon afterwards.

The reports of what God had done for me created quite a stir in the village that day. Some thought one thing, and some another. In the evening, without any announcement being made that I could learn, everybody headed for the place where they usually held their prayer meetings. My conversion had been quite a shock to many. I later learned that some time before, some members of the church had wanted to make me a particular subject of prayer, but that Mr. Gale had discouraged them, saying that he did not believe I would ever be converted. He said he had found that I knew a great deal about the faith, but that I was very hardened. He also said he was very discouraged by the fact that I led the choir and taught music to the young people. He said that they were under my influence to such a degree that he did not believe that they would ever be converted while I remained in Adams.

I found after I was converted, that some of the worst men in the place had hid behind me. One in particular, a Mr. C, who had a Christian wife, had repeatedly said to her, "If Christianity is true, why don't you convert Finney? If you Christians can convert Finney, I will believe."

An old lawyer by the name of M, who lived in Adams, heard the rumors that day and said it was all a hoax. He said I was simply trying to see what I could make Christian people believe.

However, the people rushed to the place of worship that night. I went there myself. The minister was there, and most of the influential people in the village. No one seemed ready to open the meeting but the room was totally packed. I did not wait, but got up and began by saying that I now knew that Christianity was from God. I went on and told all the important parts of my experience that day. Mr. C was present, who had promised his wife that if I was converted he would believe. Mr. M, the old lawyer, was also present. What the Lord enabled me to say seemed to take a powerful hold on the people. Mr. C got up, pushed through the crowd and went home, leaving his hat. Mr. M also left and went home, saying I was mad. "He is serious about it," he said, "there is no mistake. But he is deranged, that is clear."

As soon as I had finished speaking, pastor Gale got up and made a confession. He said he believed he had stood in the way of the church and had discouraged them when they wanted to pray for me. He also said that when he first heard that I was converted, he did not believe it. He said he had no faith. He spoke in a very humble manner.

I had never prayed in public before. But after Mr. Gale finished speaking, he called on me to pray. I did so, and found that I had a good deal of power and freedom in prayer. We had a wonderful meeting that evening, and from then on we had a meeting every night for a long time. The revival spread in every direction.

Because I had been a leader among the young people, I immediately appointed a meeting for my class, which they all attended. I went to work to see them converted, and the Lord blessed every effort that was made in a powerful way. They were converted one after the other very quickly, until only one was left.

The work spread, not only through the village, but out of the village in every direction. My heart was so full that, for more than a week, I did not feel at all like sleeping or eating. I seemed to literally have 'bread' that the world knew nothing of. I did not feel the need of food or sleep. My mind was full of the love of God to overflowing. I went on like this for quite some time until I found that I must have rest or I was in danger of losing my mind. From that point on, I was more cautious. I ate regularly and slept as much as I could.

The Word of God had wonderful power, and every day I was surprised to find that a few words spoken to an individual would stick in his heart like an arrow.

After a short time I went down to Henderson where my father lived, for a visit. He was an unconverted man and only one of the family, my youngest brother, had ever become a Christian. My father met me at the gate and said, "How are you, Charles?" I replied, "I am well, father, body and soul. But, father, you are an old man. All your children have grown up and left you and I never heard a prayer in my father's house." He dropped his head and burst into tears, and replied, "I know it, Charles. Come in and pray yourself."

We went in and prayed. My father and mother were deeply moved, and were both converted. It is possible that my mother had had a secret faith before this, but if so, none of the family ever knew about it.

I remained in the neighborhood for two or three days, and talked with everyone I met. The next Monday night they had a monthly prayer meeting in that town. The area was very much a moral wasteland, however, and Christianity was at a very low ebb. My youngest brother attended this monthly meeting, and later told me all about it.

Deacon M of the Congregational church was a quiet, feeble old man. He had a reputation as a good Christian but seldom talked about it. He led the meeting. A scripture was read, they sang a hymn, and Deacon M stood up behind his chair and led in prayer. The other people knelt down around the room.

My brother said that Deacon M began his prayer as usual in a low, feeble voice. But before long he began to raise his voice, which trembled with emotion. He started to pray with more and more intensity, until he began to rise up on his toes and come down on his heels, and then rise up on his toes and drop down on his heels again, so that they could feel the jar in the room. He continued to raise his voice. And as the spirit of prayer led him onward he began to raise his chair along with his heels, and bring that down on the floor as well. He continued to do this, and grew more and more emphatic, until it seemed that he would break the chair to bits.

In the meantime the people that were on their knees began to groan and sigh and weep, and agonize in prayer. The deacon continued to struggle on in prayer until he was almost exhausted, and when he stopped my brother said that no one in the room could get off their knees. They could only weep and confess and melt down before the Lord. From this meeting the revival spread in every direction, all over town. And so it spread from Adams in the center, through nearly all the towns in that county.

I have spoken of the conviction of Squire W in whose office I studied law. I have also said that when I was converted, it was in a grove where I went to pray. Very soon after my conversion, several other conversions occurred under similar circumstances. People went up into the grove to pray, and made their peace with God there.

When Squire W heard them tell their experience, one after the other, in our meetings, he thought to himself that he had a parlor to pray in, and that he was not going up into the woods to have the same story to tell as all the others. He strongly committed himself to this. And though it seemed such a trivial thing, yet it was a point on which his pride had been committed, and so he could not get into the kingdom of God.

I have seen quite a few cases like this over the years – where a person's pride was committed on some trivial point. In all such cases they had to yield on that issue, or they could never get into the kingdom of God. I have known people to remain for weeks in great distress, convicted by the Spirit. But they could make no progress until they yielded that particular thing to God. Mr. W was the first case of this kind that I had ever seen.

After he was converted, he said the question had often come up when he was in prayer – and that he half knew that it was pride that made him take that stand, and that kept him out of the kingdom of God. But still he was not willing to fully admit this, even to himself. He tried in every way to make himself believe, and to make God believe, that he was not proud. One night, he said, he prayed all night in his parlor that God would have mercy on him. But in the morning he felt more distressed than ever. He finally became enraged that God did not hear his prayers, and was tempted to kill himself. He was so tempted to use his penknife for that purpose, that he actually threw it as far as he could to avoid the temptation. He said that one night, while returning from a meeting, he was so convicted about his pride that he looked around for a mud puddle to kneel down in, so he could show that it was not pride which kept him from going into the woods. In this way he continued to struggle for several weeks.

But one afternoon I was sitting in our office when a young man burst in and exclaimed, "Squire W is converted!" He continued: "I went up into the woods to pray, and heard someone over in the valley shouting very loud. I went up to the brow of the hill and saw Squire W pacing to and fro and singing as loud as he could. Every so often he would stop and clap his hands with his full strength and shout, 'I will rejoice in the God of my salvation!' Then he would march and sing again, and then stop and shout and clap his hands." While the young man was telling us this, Squire W appeared, coming over the hill. As he came down he met Father T, as we called him, an aged Methodist brother. He rushed up to him, and gave him a huge bearhug. After putting him down and talking for a moment, he came rapidly towards the office. When he came in he cried, "I've got it! I've got it!" He fell on his knees and began to thank God. He then told us what had happened. He said that as soon as he gave up that point and went into the woods, it was such a relief. And when he knelt down to pray, the Spirit of God came upon him and filled him with unspeakable joy.

Towards spring the zeal of the older members of the church began to decline. I had been in the habit of rising early in the morning and praying alone in the meeting house, and I finally succeeded in getting quite a few brothers to meet me there for a morning prayer meeting. This was at a very early hour. I persuaded my minister to attend these meetings as well.

But soon they began to slacken off, so I would get up in time to go around to their houses and wake them up. Many times I went round and round, and called the brothers that I thought would be most likely to attend, and we would have a precious time of prayer. But still they attended with more and more reluctance. I was very discouraged by this.

One morning I had done the rounds, but when I got back to the meeting house there were only a few of them there. Pastor Gale was standing at the door of the church and as I came up, all at once the glory of God shone all around me, with real power. The day was just beginning to dawn. But all at once an incredible light shone into my soul, that almost made me fall to the ground. In this light it seemed as if I could see that all nature praised and worshipped God except man. It seemed to be like the brightness of the sun in every direction. It was too intense for my eyes. I remember breaking into a flood of tears because of the fact that mankind did not praise God. It was as if I experienced something of the light that blinded Paul on his way to Damascus. I surely could not have endured it for long.

When I burst into such loud weeping, Mr. Gale said, "What is the matter, Brother Finney?" I could not tell him. I found that he had seen no light, and that he saw no reason why I might be in such a state. So I said very little. I simply replied that I saw the glory of God, and that I could not bear to think of the way He was treated by men. To be honest, it was a vision of His glory that I could hardly describe in words. I wept it out. And the vision passed away and left my mind calm.

When I was a young Christian, I used to have many experiences of communing with God that cannot be described in words. And very often they would end with an impression like this: "Go, and see that you tell no-one." I did not understand this, and several times I tried to tell other Christians about these communings with God. But I soon found that it did not work trying to tell people what God was doing in my life. They could not understand it. They would look surprised and sometimes incredulous. I soon learned to keep quiet about these experiences, and to say little about them.

I used to spend a great deal of time in prayer, sometimes literally praying without ceasing. I also found it very helpful to set aside days of private fasting quite often. On those days I would seek to be entirely alone with God, and would generally wander off into the woods or get into the meeting house, or somewhere entirely by myself.

Sometimes I would pursue the wrong direction in fasting, and attempt to examine myself very introspectively, as the church taught us to do. I would try to look into my heart and examine my feelings – particularly my motives and my state of mind. When I did this, I always found that the day would pass without any real progress being made. Later I could see why. I was turning my attention away from the Lord Jesus Christ and looking at myself the whole time. But whenever I fasted and let the Spirit take His own course with me, and gave myself up to let Him lead and teach me, I always found it very beneficial. I found I could not live without the presence of God, and if at any time a cloud came over me, I could not rest, I could not study, I could not do anything until the way was totally cleared between my soul and God.

I had been very fond of my profession. But as I have said, when I was converted all was dark in that direction, and I had no pleasure in the law business. I had many urgent invitations to conduct lawsuits, but I always refused. I did not dare to trust myself in the excitement of a trial. And the business of conducting other peoples' controversies seemed odious and offensive to me.

In those early days, the Lord taught me many important truths regarding the spirit of prayer. Not long after I was converted, a woman whom I had boarded with became very sick. She was not a Christian, but her husband was. He came into our office one evening and said to me, "My wife cannot live through the night." This seemed to pierce my heart like an arrow. It came upon me like a crushing weight, which I could not understand at all. And with it came an intense desire to pray for that woman. The burden was so great that I left the office almost immediately, and went up to the meeting house to pray for her. There I struggled, but could not say much. I could only groan with groanings loud and deep.

I stayed there for quite some time in this state of mind, but got no relief. I returned to the office, but could not sit still. I could only walk the room and agonize. I returned to the meeting house again, and went through the same process of struggling. For a long time I tried to get my prayer before the Lord, but somehow words could not express it. I could only groan and weep, without being able to express what I wanted in words. I returned to the office again, and still found I was unable to rest, so I returned to the meeting house for the third time. Suddenly God gave me power to prevail. I was able to roll the burden upon Him, and I felt an assurance that the woman would not die – in fact that she would never die in her sins. I returned to the office. My mind was perfectly quiet and I soon went home to bed. Early the next morning the husband of the woman came into the office. I asked how his wife was. He said, smiling, "She's alive, and seems a lot better this morning." I replied, "Brother, she will not die with this sickness – you can be sure of it. And she will never die in her sins." I don't know how I knew this, but it was made clear to me somehow. I had no doubt that she would recover. She did, and soon became a Christian.

At first I did not understand what it was that I had gone through. But shortly afterwards, as I was discussing it with a Christian brother he said to me, "That was the travail of your soul." He pointed me to certain scriptures to help me understand.

Another experience which I had soon after this, illustrates the same truth. There was a young woman in our town who remained unconverted. Many of the Christians were concerned about her. She was a charming girl, and knew a lot about Christianity, but she remained in her sins.

One of the elders of the church and myself agreed to pray for her daily – morning, noon and night – until she was either converted or we were unable to keep it up. I found myself greatly distressed for her, more and more as I continued to pray. I soon found, however, that the elder was losing the spirit of prayer for her. But this did not discourage me. I continued to hold on to God with increasing intensity. I also took every opportunity to speak plainly and searchingly with her about her salvation.

After things had continued this way for some time, one evening I called to see her just as the sun was setting. As I came up to the door I heard a shriek from a female voice, and a scuffling and confusion inside the door. I stood and waited. The lady of the house came to the door holding part of a book which had obviously been torn in two. She was pale and very upset. She held out the book and said, "Mr. Finney, do you think my sister has become a Universalist?" The book was a defense of Universalism. Her sister had found her reading it, and tried to get it away from her. It was this struggle over the book that I had heard.

I declined to go inside. The whole thing struck me in almost the same way as the announcement that the sick woman was about to die. It loaded me down with great agony. As I returned to my room I felt as though I would almost stagger under the weight that was on my mind. I struggled and groaned and agonized, but could not present the situation before God in words, but only in groans and tears.

It seemed as if the discovery that that young woman, instead of being converted, was becoming a Universalist, horrified me to such a degree that I could not break through with my faith and get hold of God on her behalf. There seemed to be a darkness hanging over the question, as if a cloud had risen up between me and God regarding her salvation. But still the Spirit struggled inside me with 'groanings that could not be uttered'.

However, I was forced to go to bed that night without having prevailed. But as soon as it was light I awoke, and the first thought I had was to cry out to God again for that young woman. No sooner was I on my knees than the darkness gave way and He said to me, "Yes! yes!" If He had spoken with an audible voice, it could not have been more clear. It instantly relieved my burden. My mind became filled with the greatest peace and joy, and I felt completely certain that her salvation was secure.

I assumed wrongly, however, in regard to the timing, which was not something that I had really heard from God about. I expected her to be converted immediately, but she wasn't. She remained in her sins for several months. I felt disappointed at the time that she was not converted straight away, and wondered whether I had really prevailed with God on her behalf.

Soon after I was converted, the man I was boarding with who was a magistrate, was deeply convicted of sin. He had been elected a member of the state legislature. I was praying daily for him, and urging him to give his heart to God. His conviction became very deep. But still he delayed. My burden for him increased.

One afternoon several of his political friends had a long meeting with him. That evening I again tried to bring his case before God. The urgency I felt for his conversion had become almost overwhelming. In my prayer I had drawn very near to God. I do not remember ever being in more intimate communion with the Lord Jesus Christ than I was at that time. His presence was so real that I was bathed in tears of joy and gratitude and love. It was in this state of mind that I attempted to pray for my friend. But the moment I did so, my mouth was shut. I found it impossible to pray a word for him. The Lord seemed to say to me, "No, I will not hear." Anguish seized hold of me. I thought at first it was a temptation. But the door was shut in my face. I didn't know what to make of it.

The next morning I saw him, and as soon as I brought up the question of submission to God he said to me, "Mr. Finney, I'll have nothing more to do with it until I return from the legislature. I am committed to carry out certain measures in the legislature that are incompatible with Christianity, and I have promised that I will leave it alone until after I have returned from Albany."

From that moment the evening before, I had had no spirit of prayer for him at all. As soon as he told me what he had done, I understood it. I could see that his convictions were all gone, and that the Spirit of God had left him. From that time he grew more hardened than ever.

When the time came he went to the legislature, and in the Spring he returned an almost insane Universalist. I say almost insane, because instead of having formed his opinions from any evidence or argument, he told me this: "I have come to this conclusion, not because I have found it taught in the Bible, but because such a doctrine is so opposed to the carnal mind. It is a doctrine that is rejected and spoken against, which proves that it is distasteful to the carnal or unconverted mind." This was staggering to me. But everything else that I could get out of him was as wild and absurd as this. He remained in his sins, finally fell into decay, and died a dilapidated old man, in the full faith of his Universalism.

Chapter Four

LICENSED TO PREACH

As I said, in the spring the older members of the church seemed to decline in their zeal for God. This greatly distressed me and many of the other young converts. About this time I read in an article entitled, "A Revival Revived." The substance of it was that in a certain place there had been a revival during the winter, but in the spring it declined. However, when urgent prayer was made for the continued outpouring of the Spirit, the revival was powerfully revived. This article sent me into a flood of weeping.

I was boarding with Mr. Gale at the time, and I took the article to him. I was so overcome with a sense of God's goodness in hearing and answering prayer, and that He would hear and answer prayer for the revival of His work in Adams, that I went through the house weeping aloud like a child. Mr. Gale seemed surprised at my feelings, and my confidence that God would revive His work. The article made no such impression on him.

At the next meeting of the young people, I proposed that we begin a concert of prayer for the revival of God's work – that we pray in our own rooms at sunrise, noon and sunset for a whole week – and then come together again. Nothing else was done to revive the revival. But the spirit of prayer was immediately poured out powerfully on the young converts. Before the week was out I learned that some of them, while attempting to pray in their rooms, would lose all their strength and be unable to stand or even rise onto their knees. They would simply lie prostrate on the floor, and pray with unutterable groanings for the outpouring of the Spirit of God.

The Spirit was poured out, and before the week ended all the meetings were full. There was as much interest in Christianity as there had been at any time during the revival.

But about this time a mistake was made, or perhaps a sin committed, by some of the older members of the church. I learned later that quite a number of the older people resisted this new movement among the young converts. They were jealous of it. They did not know what to make of it, and felt that the young converts were out of place in being so urgent with the older members of the church. This eventually grieved the Spirit of God. It was not long before bitterness began to arise among these older members of the church. The young people held out well. As far as I know, the converts were almost universally sound, and have been thoroughly effective Christians.

In the Spring of 1822, I applied to the Presbytery to become a licensed preacher. Some of the ministers urged me to go to Princeton to study theology, but I declined. When they asked me why, I told them that my finances would not allow me to go. This was true, but they said they would pay my expenses. Still I refused to go, and when asked, I plainly told them that I would not put myself under such an influence as they had been under. I felt they had been wrongly educated, and they were not my ideal of what a minister of Christ should be. I told them this reluctantly, but I could not honestly hold it back. They appointed my pastor to supervise my studies. He offered me the use of his library, and said he would help me with my theological studies.

But as far as he was concerned, my studies were virtually nothing but controversy. I could not go along with his views on the new birth, atonement, faith, repentance or any of the basic doctrines. But he held his views quite fiercely and he sometimes seemed impatient because I did not receive them without question.

He used to insist that if I tried to reason on these subjects, I would probably lose my faith. He reminded me that some of the students at Princeton had left as atheists, because they used their reason, and would not simply accept the teaching of the professors. He warned me repeatedly that as a minister I would never be any use unless I accepted the truth – meaning the truth as he believed and taught it.

I'm sure I was quite willing to believe what I found taught in the Bible, and told him so. We used to have many long discussions, and I would often leave his study deeply depressed and discouraged, saying to myself, "I cannot accept these views, come what may. I cannot believe they are taught in the Bible." Several times I was on the point of giving up my studies altogether.

There was only one member of the church that I talked to openly about all this, and that was Elder H, a very godly, praying man. He had been taught Princeton theology, and was quite a strong Calvinist. But as we discussed these things he became convinced that I was right. He would visit often and pray with me, to strengthen me in my studies, and in my discussions with Mr. Gale. He helped convince me that, come what may, I would preach the Gospel.

Several times he found me when I was in a state of deep depression after coming from Mr. Gale's study. At such times he would go with me to my room, and sometimes we would pray until late at night – crying out to God for light and strength and faith. He lived more than three miles from the village and often he stayed with me until ten or eleven at night, and then walked home. The dear old man! I have reason to believe that he prayed for me daily as long as he lived.

After I entered the ministry and great opposition was raised to my preaching, I met Elder H one time, and he alluded to the opposition and said, "My soul is so burdened that I pray for you day and night. But I am sure that God will answer. Keep on, brother Finney. The Lord will give you victory."

The time finally came when the presbytery gathered in Adams to examine me and decide if they could license me to become a preacher. This was in March 1824. I expected a severe trial, but I found them quite friendly. I think the obvious blessing that had accompanied my teaching and preaching made them more cautious than they would otherwise have been in getting into any controversy with me. During my examination they avoided asking any questions that would tend to bring my views into collision with theirs. They voted unanimously to license me.

It was at this meeting that I first saw Rev. Daniel Nash, who is generally known as "Father Nash." He was a member of the presbytery. At that time he was in a rather cold and backslidden state. But I will be mentioning him again before long.

The Sunday after I was licensed, I preached for pastor Gale. When I came out of the pulpit he said to me, "Mr. Finney, I will be truly ashamed if you make it known that you studied theology with me." This was so much like him and what he had said repeatedly to me, that I made little or no reply. I hung my head, feeling discouraged, and walked away.

Later he saw things very differently, and told me that he blessed the Lord that in all our discussion he had not had the least influence to change my views. He apologised and said that if I had listened to him it would have ruined me as a minister.

The fact is that Mr. Gale's education for the ministry had been totally defective. He had imbibed a set of beliefs that were a straitjacket for him. He could accomplish very little or nothing if he carried these out. I had the use of his library and searched it thoroughly on all the questions of theology that came up. And the more I studied the books, the more I was dissatisfied.

I had been used to the logical reasoning of the judges in my law books. But when I went to Mr. Gale's books I found them very unsatisfactory. I'm sure it was not because I was opposed to the truth, but rather because their positions were unsound and not properly proven. They often seemed to state one thing and prove another, and frequently fell short of logically proving anything.

Often when I left Mr. Gale, I would go to my room and spend a long time on my knees with my Bible, crying out to God to teach me His view on these things. I had nowhere to go but directly to the Scriptures.

Slowly I developed my own views. I knew I could not accept pastor Gale's teachings. After a lot of study and prayer, I formed views that were in opposition to them, which seemed to me to be truly Biblical.

Not only were Mr. Gale's theological views the kind that would cripple any ministry, but his practical views were just as bad. This is why he predicted all kinds of disaster for my future. He assured me that the Spirit of God would not approve or cooperate with my ministry, and that if I spoke to people the way I intended to, they would never listen. They would become offended and stay away. And unless I wrote out my sermons I would quickly become stale and boring. He told me I would divide and scatter instead of building up the people. To sum up, I found his views to be almost the exact opposite of mine in every practical way.

It is no surprise that he was shocked at my views on preaching the Gospel. With his background, that is what you would expect. He followed his views with very little result. I pursued mine, and by the blessing of God the results were the opposite of what he predicted. When this became clear, it completely overturned his theology. At first, this destroyed his hope as a Christian, but after awhile it totally transformed his preaching.

However, there was another defect in Brother Gale's education, which I regard as very basic. If he had ever been converted to Christ, he had failed to receive the anointing of the Holy Spirit that would make him a powerful preacher and see souls converted. He had fallen short of receiving the baptism of the Holy Spirit, which is totally essential to success in ministry.

When Christ sent His apostles to go and preach, He told them to wait in Jerusalem until they were 'endued with power from on high.' This power, as everyone knows, was the baptism of the Holy Spirit poured out upon them on the day of Pentecost. It was totally essential for success in their ministry. I don't believe this baptism was simply the power to work miracles. The power to work miracles and the gift of tongues were given as signs to prove that God had sent them. But the baptism itself was a holy purifying, an anointing, giving them light and filling them with faith, love, peace and power – so that their words would pierce into the hearts of God's enemies, quick and powerful, like a two-edged sword. This is totally basic for success in ministry, and I have often been surprised that to this day so little emphasis is placed upon it. Without the direct teaching of the Holy Spirit, nobody will ever be much good at preaching the Gospel.

As I said, Mr. Gale later came to the conclusion that he had never been converted. I have no doubt that he was a good and sincere man. But his education was sadly defective – theologically and in every way. And from what I saw of his spiritual state, he did not seem to have made his peace with God when I sat under his ministry.

But do not think for a moment that I did not love and respect Mr. Gale. I did both. He and I remained the firmest friends until the day he died. I have told you about these things because, sadly, I think they apply to many ministers even today. I believe that their practical views of preaching the Gospel, whatever their theological views may be, are terribly defective. And their lack of the power of the Holy Spirit is a radical defect in their preparation for ministry. I do not say this in a nasty way. But it as a tragic fact that has deeply saddened me over the years. The more I have seen, the more I have become convinced that with all their training, there is still a lack of knowledge of the best way to present the Gospel, and a terrible lack of the power of the Holy Spirit.

Chapter Five

REVIVAL MINISTRY WIDENS

Because I had no regular training, I did not expect to minister in large towns or cities, or preach to sophisticated congregations. I intended to go into the new settlements and preach in schoolhouses, barns and groves as best I could. So after being licensed to preach, I went into the northern part of Jefferson County, and began my ministry at Evans' Mills in the town of Le Ray.

I started preaching in the stone schoolhouse at Evans' Mills. The people seemed very interested, and crowded in to hear me preach. They complimented my preaching and the little Congregational church had hopes that there would be a revival. Convictions occurred under every sermon that I preached, but there was still no general conviction amongst the people.

I was very unhappy with this. At one of the evening meetings, having preached there quite a few times, I told the people that I had come there to secure the salvation of their souls. I said I knew my preaching was highly complimented by them, but I had not come there to please them, but to bring them to repentance. I didn't care whether they liked my preaching or not, if in the end they still rejected my Master. I said I could not spend my time with them unless they were going to accept the Gospel. I quoted the words of Abraham's servant: "Now will you deal kindly and truly with my master? If you will, tell me; and if not, tell me, that I may turn to the right hand or the left." I insisted that I must know what course they wanted to pursue. If they did not want to become Christians, I wanted to know it so that I did not waste my time. I said to them, "You admit that what I preach is the Gospel. You say you believe it. Now will you receive it? Are you going to accept it or reject it?

You must have some opinion about it. You admit that I preach the truth, so I believe you are obliged to obey it. So will you meet this obligation? Will you do what you know you should? If not, tell me, so that I may turn to the right hand or the left."

After turning this over until I saw that they understood it well, and looked very surprised at my way of putting it, I then said to them, "Now I must know your decision. I want you who have made up your minds to become Christians right now, to stand up. But on the other hand, those of you who have decided not to become Christians, and want Christ to understand this, should sit still." After making this plain so I knew they understood it, I then said: "You who are willing to pledge to me and to Christ, that you will immediately make your peace with God, please stand up. On the other hand, you that are committed not to accept Christ – please sit still." They looked at one another and at me, and they all sat still, just as I expected.

After looking at them for a few moments, I said, "Then you are committed. You have taken your stand. You have rejected Christ and His Gospel. You are witnesses against one another, and God is a witness against you all. You may remember as long as you live, that you have publicly committed yourselves against the Savior, and said, 'We will not have this man, Jesus Christ, to reign over us.'" This is the substance of what I said to them, as near as I can recall.

When I spoke to them this way they began to look angry, and arose en masse and started for the door. When they began to move, I paused. They turned to see why. I said, "I am sorry for you and I will preach to you one more time, tomorrow night."

They all left except Deacon McC who was from the Baptist church there. I saw that the Congregationalists were in shock. They were few in number and very weak in faith. It seemed that the people from both churches who were there, except Deacon McC, were in despair – thinking it was all over. But Deacon McC came up and took me by the hand and said, "Brother Finney, you have got them.

They cannot rest under this. The Christians are all discouraged, but I'm not. I believe you have done the very thing that needed to be done, and we will see the results." I thought so myself, of course. I intended to place them in a position that would make them tremble at what they had done. But that evening and the next day they were full of anger. Deacon McC and I agreed to spend the next day in fasting and prayer – separately in the morning and together in the afternoon. I learned that the people were threatening to tar and feather me, or something similar. Some of them cursed me and said that I had put them under oath that they would not serve God. They said I had drawn them into a public pledge to reject Christ and His Gospel. This was pretty much what I expected. In the afternoon Deacon McC and I went into the woods and spent the whole afternoon in prayer. As evening fell the Lord gave us a promise of victory. Both of us felt that we had prevailed with God, and that the power of God would be unleashed among the people that night.

The meeting time arrived, and we left the woods and went into the village. The people were already rushing to the place of worship, and those that were not there already left their shops and offices, or threw down their golf clubs, and packed the place until it could hold no more.

I had not even thought about what I would preach. In fact, this was common with me at the time. The Holy Spirit was on me, and I felt confident that when the time came for action I would know what to preach. As soon as the place was packed so that no more could get in, I stood up and without any singing, opened with this Scripture: "Say to the righteous that it shall be well with him; for they shall eat the fruit of their doings. Woe to the wicked! It shall be ill with him; for the reward of his hands shall be given him." The Spirit of God came upon me with such power that it was like opening a gun battery on them. For more than an hour – perhaps for an hour and a half – the Word of God came through me in a way that I could see was carrying all before it. It was like a fire, or a hammer breaking rock – a sword that pierced to 'the dividing asunder of soul and spirit'. I saw that a general conviction was spreading over the whole congregation. Many of them could not hold up their heads. I did not call for any reversal of the stand they had taken the night before, or for any commitment of any kind. I simply took it for granted during the whole sermon, that they were committed against the Lord. Then I announced that there would be another meeting and dismissed the congregation.

As the people went out I saw a woman in the arms of some of her friends who were supporting her, and I went to see what was the matter. I thought she must have fainted. But I soon found that she was not fainting, but that she could not speak. There was a look of great anguish on her face. I advised the women to take her home and pray with her, and see what the Lord would do. They informed me that she was Miss G, sister of a well-known missionary, and that she had been a member of the church for several years.

That evening I accepted an invitation, and went home with a family whom I had not stayed with before. Early in the morning I found that I had been sent for several times in the night, to visit families where there were people who were in terrible spiritual distress. Everywhere I went that morning I found a state of wonderful conviction of sin and alarm for their souls.

After lying speechless for about sixteen hours, Miss G's mouth was opened, and a new song was given to her. She was taken from 'the pit of miry clay', and her feet were 'set upon a rock.' This led to a great deal of soul-searching amongst the members of the church. She said she had been totally deceived. For eight years she had been a member of the church, and thought she was a Christian, but during the sermon the night before she saw that she had never known the true God. When God's true character was presented, her hope disappeared 'like a moth,' as she put it. She said that such a picture of God's holiness was presented that it swept away her false assurance of salvation in a moment.

There was an old man there who was an atheist. He was very angry at the revival. Every day I heard about his cursing and blaspheming, but took no public notice of it. He refused to attend any of the meetings. But at the height of his opposition, while sitting at his table one morning, he suddenly fell out of his chair in a kind of fit. A doctor was called and said that he had only a short time to live. If he had anything to say, he needed to say it at once. He had just enough strength and time to stammer out, "Don't let Finney pray over my corpse." This was the last of his opposition in that place.

I met Father Nash again, whom I had last seen at the meeting of the presbytery. He had been ill with inflamed eyes, and for several weeks was shut up in a dark room. He could neither read nor write, and gave himself almost entirely to prayer. He went through a massive overhauling of his whole Christian walk, and as soon as he was able to see, he went all-out to win souls for Christ.

When he came to Evans' Mills he was full of the power of prayer. He was a totally different man from what he had been. He told me that he had a prayer list, with the names of people that he prayed for every day, and sometimes many times a day. I found that his gift of prayer was wonderful, and his faith almost miraculous.

There was a man by the name of D, who owned a tavern in a corner of the village. All the opposers of the revival would meet there. The bar was full of blasphemy and he himself was an ungodly and abusive man. He would take great pleasure in swearing and blaspheming whenever he saw a Christian. One of the young converts lived almost across the street, and he told me that he wanted to sell up and move away, because every time D saw him he would come out and swear and curse and say everything he could to belittle him. I don't think he had been to any of our meetings.

Father Nash heard us speak of this Mr. D as a hard case, and immediately put his name on his prayer list. He stayed in town a day or two, and then went on his way.

Not long afterwards during a crowded evening meeting, who should come in but this notorious Mr. D? His entrance caused quite a stir. People were worried that he had come in to make a disturbance. In fact, some people actually got up and left. I knew his face, and kept my eye on him. But I soon realized that he had not come in to oppose, but seemed to be in great anguish. He squirmed in his seat, and seemed very uneasy. He stood up and tremblingly asked if he could say a few words. I told him that he could. He then made one of the most heart-broken confessions I have ever heard. His confession seemed to cover his treatment of God, his treatment of Christians and the revival, and of everything good.

This broke up the hard ground in many hearts. It was the most powerful thing that could have happened at that moment to propel the revival forward. Mr. D became a strong Christian and rid his barroom of all the blasphemy and so-on that had taken place there. From that time on, a prayer meeting was held in his barroom nearly every night.

Chapter Six

THE FLAME SPREADS

Not far from Evans' Mills was a settlement where there was a German church that had quite a large membership, but no preacher and no regular meetings. Once a year a minister came and administered baptism and the Lord's Supper. He would confirm their children, and after they had received communion they took it for granted that they were Christians, and that all was safe.

They asked me to go there and preach. I agreed, and I preached the first time from this Scripture: "Without holiness no man shall see the Lord."

The settlement turned out en masse, and the schoolhouse where they worshipped was filled to overflowing. They could understand English well. I began by showing what holiness is not. Under this heading I took everything that they considered to be Christianity and showed that it was not holiness at all. Secondly I showed what holiness is. Thirdly, I showed them what is meant by 'seeing the Lord'. And after that, why those that had no holiness could never be admitted into God's presence or be accepted by Him. I then finished with some pointed comments that were designed to really make the subject go home. And it did go home by the power of the Holy Spirit. The sword of the Lord slew them on the right hand and on the left.

Within a few days the whole settlement was under conviction. The elders of the church and everyone were in anguish, feeling that they had no holiness. At their request I appointed a meeting for those who were seeking God. This was during their harvest time. I held the meeting at one o'clock in the afternoon, and found the place literally packed. People had thrown down their harvesting tools and come to the meeting.

This revival among the Germans resulted in the conversion of the whole church, I believe, and nearly the whole community. It was one of the most interesting revivals I ever saw.

While I was ministering there, the presbytery were called together to ordain me, which they did.

During the revival at Evans' Mills, there was a wonderful spirit of prayer among the Christians, and true unity. The little Congregational church, as soon as they saw the results of my preaching, recovered and rallied behind the revival as best they could. They really grew in grace and in the knowledge of Christ during that revival.

I placed great emphasis on prayer as an essential prerequisite to revival. The atonement of Christ, His death and resurrection, repentance, faith and all the other basic doctrines were discussed as thoroughly as possible, and made effective by the power of the Holy Spirit.

The methods I used were simply preaching, prayer meetings, private prayer, personal conversation, and special meetings for those who were seeking God. No other methods were used. And there was no appearance of fanaticism or division or heresy. In fact, nothing ever resulted from that revival that was questionable or damaging, as far as I know.

However, there was quite intense opposition at times. One thing that added to this opposition was that the area was a kind of "burnt district" (spiritually speaking). A few years earlier a wild excitement had passed through, which they called a revival, but which turned out to be false. Apparently emotionalism had run so high that it caused a terrible reaction, and many were left with the impression that Christianity was a mere delusion. Thus they felt justified in opposing anything that even looked like a revival.

I found that it had left some ridiculous practices behind amongst the Christians. For example, in the prayer meetings every believer felt it was their duty to testify for Christ. They must "take up the cross" and say something in the meeting. One of them might say: "I have a duty to perform. I testify that Christianity is good, though I must admit I do not enjoy it at present. I have nothing in particular to say, but I hope you will all pray for me." Then another person would stand up and say something to the same effect: "Christianity is good but I do not enjoy it. I have nothing else to say, but I must do my duty. I hope you will all pray for me." Thus the time would pass. Of course the unbelievers would mock these meetings.

It was quite ridiculous. But this is what they thought a prayer meeting was supposed to be like, so to get rid of it I had to make every meeting a 'preaching' meeting. When we met together, I would begin by singing, and then would pray myself. I would then call on one or two others to pray, naming them. Then I would read a Scripture and talk for awhile. When I saw that this had made an impact, I would stop and ask one or two to pray that the message would take hold in their hearts. I would then continue with my talk and after awhile, stop again and ask one or two more to pray. This is how I avoided opening up the meetings for their 'testimonies.' They could then go home without feeling that they had neglected their duty in not testifying for God. And so we got over that silly method of holding meetings that created so much laughter and ridicule among unbelievers.

After the revival took thorough hold, opposition totally ceased as far as I could tell. I spent over six months there and at Antwerp, dividing my time between the two places, and towards the end I heard nothing of open opposition.

During the six months that I ministered in that area I rode on horseback from settlement to settlement in various directions, and preached the Gospel whenever I had the opportunity. When I left Adams my health had been quite run down. I had coughed blood, and my friends thought that I would only live a short time. Mr.

Gale told me not to attempt to preach more than once a week, and to make sure that I did not speak for more than half an hour at a time. But instead, I visited from house to house, attended prayer meetings and preached every day and almost every night, for that entire time. Before six months were out, my health was totally restored, my lungs were sound, and I could preach for two and a half hours or longer, without feeling tired at all. I think my sermons generally averaged around two hours. I preached in the open air, I preached in barns, I preached in schoolhouses, and a glorious revival spread over that whole region.

During the early part of my ministry especially, I used to get knocked back by other preachers because of the way that I preached. They would disapprove of me for illustrating my ideas using everyday situations, as I often did. Among farmers and mechanics and other working people, I borrowed my illustrations from their various occupations. I tried to use language that they would understand – words that were in common use.

Before I was converted it was different. In writing and speaking, I sometimes used ornate language. But when I came to preach the Gospel, I was so anxious to be understood that I tried to express my thoughts with the simplest language I could.

Ministers would say to me, "Why don't you use events from ancient history, and take a more dignified way of illustrating your ideas?" I told them I didn't want the illustration itself to occupy peoples' minds, but rather the truth that I was trying to get across. I said that my aim was not to create a style of oratory that would soar above the heads of the people, but to make myself understood.

They used to complain that I let down the dignity of the pulpit, that I was a disgrace to the ministerial profession, that I talked like a lawyer at the bar, and that I talked to the people in a colloquial manner. They complained that I said "you" instead of preaching about sin and sinners and saying "they". They also told me that I said "hell" with such emphasis that I often shocked people. They said I urged people to respond as if they might not have a moment to live, and sometimes they said that I condemned people. After I had preached for some time and God had poured out His blessing everywhere I went, I used to say to ministers that I did not dare to make the changes that they wanted. I said, "Show me the fruits of your ministry. If you can prove by your results that you have found a better way, then I will adopt your views." I would say to them: "I want to improve all I can, but I will never adopt your way of preaching unless I see evidence that you are right and I am wrong."

They would often complain that I was guilty of repetition in my preaching. I would take the same thought and turn it over and over, and illustrate it in various ways. I told them that I felt it was necessary to do this, to make myself understood. Then they would say that the educated people in my congregation would lose interest. But the facts soon silenced them. They found that under my preaching, judges and lawyers and educated men were converted in their droves, but under their methods such a thing almost never occurred.

Chapter Seven

COMMENTS ON THE EDUCATION OF PREACHERS

In what I say on this subject I hope my brothers will not think I mean them any disrespect. I have always taken their criticisms kindly, and given them credit for good intentions. Now I am an old man, and many of my views and methods are known to the public. Is it out of place for me to speak freely to the ministry on this subject? In reply to their objections, I have sometimes told them what a judge of the Supreme Court told me: "Ministers do not use common sense. They are afraid of repetition. They use terminology that is not understood by the common people. Their illustrations are not taken from everyday situations. If lawyers did that, then they would destroy themselves and their case. When I was at the bar I used to take it for granted that I would have to repeat my main arguments about as many times as the number of people in the jury-box. I learned that unless I did, I would lose my case. The aim is to get a verdict before the jury leaves the box, not to display our oratory and then let them go. We have to get a verdict. So we have to be understood. If ministers would do this, the effects of their preaching would be hugely different from what they are now."

I never bore any grudge towards other ministers for the rough way they often treated me. I knew they were only trying to help. One time a well-known temperance lecturer from Connecticut came down to hear me preach. He was indignant at the way in which I "let down the dignity of the pulpit." He insisted that I should not be allowed to preach until I had a proper ministerial education. He said I should stop preaching and go to Princeton immediately to learn theology.

I don't want to give the impression that I thought that my views or methods were perfect, for I had no such thought. I was aware that I was but a child, so to speak. I had not been to the higher schools of learning, so I never had any higher ambition than to go into new settlements and places where the Gospel was not being preached. I was often surprised, in the first year of my preaching, that educated people found my preaching so compelling. This was more than I had expected. In fact it was more than I had dared to hope.

But the more I saw the results of my preaching, the more I could see that God had led me and taught me, and given me the right way to go about winning souls. I know it must have been God who taught me, because I never obtained these principles from man. I have often thought that, like Paul, I was not taught the Gospel by man, but by the Spirit of Christ Himself. And He taught me in a way that was so clear and strong, that no argument of my ministerial brothers had any weight with me at all.

I have to say this as a matter of duty. For I am still totally convinced that to a large extent the schools are ruining the ministers. Preachers these days have wonderful facilities for obtaining information on all theological questions, and are vastly more learned, so far as theological, historical and Biblical learning is concerned, than perhaps any age in history. Yet with all their learning, they do not know how to use it. They are, to a great extent, like David in Saul's armor. A man can never learn to preach except by preaching.

Ministers need one thing above all others, and that is singleness of eye. If they feel they have a reputation to protect, they will do little good. Many years ago a pastor friend took a break for his health's sake, and employed a young man just out of seminary to preach while he was away. This young man wrote and preached as majestic sermons as he could. The pastor's wife finally had to say to him, "You are preaching over the heads of our people. They do not understand your language or your illustrations. You bring too much learning into the pulpit." He replied, "I am a young man. I am cultivating a style. I am trying to prepare myself to minister to an educated congregation. I cannot descend to your people. I must cultivate an elevated style." I have never seen this man's name connected with any revival, amongst all the great revivals we have had since then, and I never expect to, unless his views are radically changed.

I could name ministers who are still alive today who were deeply ashamed of me when I first began to preach because I was so undignified in the pulpit, used such common language and spoke to the people with such directness.

I was aware from the start that I would meet with opposition, and that there was a wide gulf between my views and the views of other ministers. I never really felt like one of them, or that they regarded me as truly belonging to their fraternity. I was bred a lawyer. I came straight from the law office into the pulpit, and talked to the people as I would have spoken to a jury.

Any thinking person will see it as infinitely out of place to use the language of learning and rhetoric when immortal souls are on the line, hanging on the edge of everlasting death. Men do not speak that way when there is a real emergency. When a city is on fire, the fire captain does not read his men an essay or a fine piece of rhetoric. It is a matter of urgency, and he has to make every word count.

This is the way it always is when men are urgent and serious. Their language is pointed, direct and simple. Their sentences are short and powerful. They appeal for direct action. This is the reason why the uneducated Methodist preachers and the serious Baptist preachers always made a much greater impact than our most learned theologians. And they still do today. The passionate preaching of a common exhorter will often move a congregation far more than any kind of cultivated rhetoric. Great sermons lead the people to praise the preacher. Good preaching leads the people to praise the Savior.

People have often said to me: "You do not preach. You talk to the people." A man in London went home from one of our meetings deeply convicted. His wife asked him, "Have you been to hear Mr. Finney preach?" He replied: "I have been to Mr. Finney's meeting. He doesn't preach. He only explains what other people preach." I have heard this kind of comment again and again. People say, "Anybody could preach like you. You just talk to the people. You talk as if you were at home, sitting in the living room." Others have said: "It seemed as if Mr. Finney had taken me to one side, and was talking with me face to face."

Ministers usually avoid preaching directly to the people. They will preach to them about others, and the sins of others, but rarely will they ever say: "You are guilty of these sins, and the Lord requires this of you." They often preach 'about' the Gospel instead of preaching the Gospel. They often preach 'about' sinners instead of preaching to them. They go to great lengths to avoid being personal. But I have always gone down a different line than this. I have often said, "Do not think that I am talking about anybody else. I am talking to you and you and you."

Ministers told me at first that people would never put up with this – that they would get up and leave, and never come back. But they were mistaken. A lot depends on the spirit in which it is said. If it is done in the spirit of love, with an honest desire for their very best, there are very few who will continue to resent it. At the time they may feel rebuked and upset, but deep down they know that they needed it, and it will ultimately do them good.

I have often said to people, when I saw that they looked offended: "Now you resent this and you will go away saying that you're not coming back – but you will. Your own convictions are on my side. You know that what I'm telling you is true, and that I'm saying it for your own good – and you cannot continue to resent it." And I have always found this to be true.

My experience has been that honesty is the best policy for a preacher. People are not fools. They have little respect for a man who will go into the pulpit and preach smooth things. There is a part of them that despises it.

I do not spend hours and days writing my sermons, but my mind is always pondering the truths of the Gospel, and the best way to preach them. I move around amongst the people and find out what they most need to hear. Then, with the help of the Holy Spirit, I choose the topic for my sermon. I think deeply about it, pray over it and get my mind full of it – and then go and pour it out to the people. With a written sermon, after the preacher has written it down there is little need to think or pray much more about it. He may read it over on a Saturday evening or Sunday morning, but he does not feel the need to be powerfully anointed, that his mouth may be opened and filled with arguments from above. He is comfortable in the fact that he only has to use his eyes and his voice, and he can preach. Thus the message is not necessarily new or fresh – an anointed message direct from God.

I truly believe that I have studied a lot more because I have not written out my sermons. I have been forced to become extremely familiar with my subject, to fill my mind with it, and then go and pour it out to the people. All I do is sketch the briefest outline before I start.

Unless preachers actually try this kind of preaching, unless they begin to simply talk to the people, keeping their hearts full of truth and of the Holy Spirit, they can never become spontaneous preachers.

For about the first twelve years of my ministry I never wrote a word, and most of the time had to preach without any preparation at all, except what I got in prayer. Often I went into the pulpit without even knowing what Scripture I would preach from, or anything that I would say. I relied completely on the Holy Spirit to open up the whole subject to my mind, and I have never preached with greater success or power. If I did not preach by divine inspiration, I don't know how I preached. It was very common, and has been during my whole ministry, for the subject to open up to my mind in a way that surprised even me. It seemed that I could see with tremendous clarity just what I needed to say, and whole platoons of thoughts, words and illustrations came to me as fast as I could deliver them. When I first began to make outlines, I made them after, and not before I preached – to record the thoughts that God had given me. But I found that I could never re-use these old outlines anyway, without remodeling them and getting a fresh perspective from the Holy Spirit. I almost always get my sermon topics on my knees in prayer. And I have often found that when the Holy Spirit gives me something to preach, it comes so strongly that it literally makes me tremble, so I have great difficulty in writing. I find that such sermons always tell with great power upon the people.

Some of the most powerful sermons I have ever preached were actually received just as the meeting was about to begin. I am telling you this to give glory to God, and not to any talents of my own. Let no-one think that these powerful sermons were produced by my own brain or of my own heart, unassisted by the Holy Spirit. They were not mine, but came from the Holy Spirit within me.

And let no-one say that this is claiming a higher inspiration than is promised to every preacher. For I believe that all ministers are called to preach under a mighty anointing of the Holy Spirit. What else did Christ mean when He said: "If any man believes in me, out of his belly shall flow rivers of living water"? Every preacher should be so filled with the Holy Spirit that all who hear them are convinced that God is in them of a truth.

Chapter Eight

REVIVAL IN ANTWERP

I must tell you about the revival in Antwerp, a village north of Evans' mills. I arrived there in April and found that no Christian meetings of any kind were held in the town. There was a Presbyterian church there, consisting of a few members. They had tried to keep a meeting going in the village. But the elder who conducted their Sunday meetings lived about five miles away, and had to pass through a Universalist settlement. The Universalists had broken up the village meeting by making it impossible for Deacon R to get through their settlement to the meetings. They would even take off the wheels of his carriage. Finally the opposition got so bad that he gave up and all Christian meetings in the village ceased.

A lady agreed to open her house for a meeting that evening. So I went out and invited people, and about thirteen showed up. I preached to them and then said that if I could get the use of the village school house, I would preach on the Sunday. I got the permission of the trustees, and the next day an invitation was circulated among the people for a meeting on Sunday morning.

In walking around the village I heard a tremendous amount of profanity. I don't think I had ever heard so much in any one place before. Whether they were playing ball or doing business, it seemed as if the people were continually cursing and swearing and damning each other. I felt almost like I had arrived on the borders of hell. I had an awful feeling as I walked around the village on Saturday. The very atmosphere itself seemed poisonous and a kind of terror took hold of me.

I gave myself to prayer on Saturday, and finally this answer came:

"Be not afraid, but speak... for I am with you, and no-one will hurt you. For I have many people in this city." This completely relieved me of all fear. However, I found that the Christians in town really were afraid that something serious might happen if meetings were started up again. I spent almost all of Saturday in prayer, but walked around the village enough to see that the invitation that had been sent out was creating quite a stir.

On Sunday morning I went up into the woods where I could be alone with God, and spent a great deal of time in prayer. However, I did not find any relief, so I went back there a second time. But still the burden increased. So I went back a third time, and then the answer came. I found that it was time for the meeting and went straight to the schoolhouse. I found it totally packed. I had my pocket Bible in my hand, and read them this verse: "God so loved the world that he gave his only begotten son, that whosoever believes in him should not perish but have everlasting life." I can't remember much of my sermon, but I know that my main point was the treatment that God received in return for His love. The subject affected me deeply, and as I preached I poured out my soul and my tears together.

Several men were there that I had heard using the most awful profanity the day before. I pointed them out in the meeting and told the congregation what they had said – how they called on God to damn each other. Indeed, I let loose my whole heart upon them. I told them that they seemed to howl blasphemy in the streets like hell-hounds and it seemed to me that I had arrived on the very edge of hell. Everybody knew that what I said was true, and they quailed under it. They did not seem offended. The people wept about as much as I did myself. I don't think there was a dry eye in the house.

Mr. C, the landlord, had refused to open the meeting house in the morning. But as soon as this first service closed, he stood up and said that he would open the meeting house in the afternoon. The people scattered and carried the information in every direction. Thus, in the afternoon the meeting house was nearly as crowded as the schoolhouse had been in the morning. Everybody was at the meeting, and the Lord let me loose upon them in a powerful way. My preaching seemed to be something new. It seemed as if I could rain hail and love upon them at the same time – or in other words, that I could rain upon them hail, in love. It seemed as if my love for God, and the abuse that they heaped upon Him, sharpened my mind to the most intense agony. I felt like rebuking them with all my heart, and yet with a compassion that they could not mistake. I never heard them accuse me of severity but I probably never spoke with more severity in my life.

Most of the population became deeply convicted. From that day on, whenever I appointed a meeting anywhere in the area the people would throng to hear. The revival spread with great power. On Sundays I preached twice in the village church, attended a prayer meeting in between, and usually found a schoolhouse somewhere to preach in at five o'clock in the afternoon.

On the third Sunday that I preached there, an old man came up to me. He asked if I would go and preach in a schoolhouse about three miles distant, saying that they had never had any Christian meetings there. He wanted me to come as soon as I could. I decided on the next day, Monday, at five o'clock in the afternoon. It was a warm day. I left my horse in the village, and decided to walk down. However, because I had preached so hard on the Sunday, I became exhausted even before I reached the place. I kicked myself for not taking my horse.

But at the appointed time I found the schoolhouse full, and I could only get a standing-place near the open door. They sang, but I can't really call it singing. What it amounted to was that each one bawled in his own way. I had been a music teacher, and their horrible discord distressed me so much that I put both hands over my ears, and held them with my full strength. But even that did not shut out the discords. When they were finished I fell down on my knees, almost in a state of desperation, and began to pray. The Lord opened the windows of heaven and the spirit of prayer came down upon me. I was able to pour my whole heart out in prayer.

I had not even thought about what to preach, but waited to see the congregation. As soon as I had finished praying I got up from my knees and quoted this Scripture: "Quick, get out of this place, for the Lord will destroy this city." I said I did not know exactly where that passage was from, but I told them roughly where they could find it. Then I went on to explain it. I told them how incredibly evil the city of Sodom became, and what sinful practices they fell into. I told them that the Lord had decided to destroy Sodom, and visited Abraham and told him what He was going to do. He promised Abraham that if He found ten righteous people in the city He would spare it. But He actually found that there was just one righteous person there, and that was Lot. So God's angels said to Lot, "Whatever you have in the city, get it out... because the Lord has sent us to destroy it."

While I was relating these facts the people looking as if they were getting angry. Many of the men were in their shirt sleeves and they looked as if they wanted to rush forward and teach me a lesson with their fists. I saw their strange looks, but I could not understand what I was saying that had offended them. But it seemed as if their anger rose higher and higher as I continued the story. As soon as I had finished, I turned to them and said that I understood they had never had a Christian meeting in that place, and so I took it for granted that they were ungodly people. I pressed this home upon them with more and more energy, with my heart so full it was almost bursting.

I had only been speaking to them in this direct way for about quarter of an hour, when all at once an awful solemnity seemed to settle down upon them. The congregation began to fall from their seats in every direction and cry for mercy. If I had had a sword in each hand, I could not have cut them off their seats as fast as they fell. Nearly the whole congregation were either on their knees or on their faces in less than two minutes from this first shock that fell upon them. Everyone who was able to speak at all, prayed for himself.

Of course I had to stop preaching, because they no longer paid any attention. I saw the old man who had invited me there to preach, sitting in the middle of the room and looking around with utter amazement. I raised my voice almost to a scream to make him hear, and pointing to him said, "Can't you pray?" He fell on his knees, and with a loud voice poured his heart out to God. But the people paid no attention. I then spoke as loud as I could, and tried to make them listen. I said, "You are not in hell yet. Now let me direct you to Christ." For a few moments I tried to hold forth the Gospel to them, but scarcely any of them paid any attention. My heart was so full of joy at such a scene that I could hardly contain myself. It was with great difficulty that I restrained myself from shouting and giving glory to God.

As soon as I got my emotions under control, I turned to a young man who was close to me and was busy praying for himself. I put my hand on his shoulder to get his attention, and spoke in his ear about Jesus' salvation. As soon as I got his focus onto the cross of Christ, he believed, was calm and quiet for a minute or two, and then broke out praying for the others. I then turned to another person and did the same thing, with the same result. Then another, and another.

I kept on like this until I found that the time had come for me to go to another appointment in the village. I told them this, and asked the old man who had invited me there to take charge of the meeting. He did so. But there were too many wounded souls to dismiss the meeting, and so it was held all night. In the morning there were still people there that could not get away. They were carried to a house in the neighborhood so school could start. In the afternoon they sent for me again, because they still couldn't break up the meeting.

When I went down there the second time, I found out why they had become so angry during my sermon the day before. I learned that the place was called Sodom, which I did not know – and that there was only one godly man in the place, and they called him Lot. This was the old man who had invited me there. The people assumed that I had chosen my subject and preached to them that way because they were so evil as to be called Sodom. It was an amazing coincidence, but as far as I was concerned it was completely accidental.

Although revival came upon them so suddenly and powerfully, the converts were sound and the work was permanent and genuine. I never heard of any disastrous reaction taking place.

I have spoken of the Universalists who prevented Deacon R from attending meetings by taking off the wheels of his carriage. When the revival got to full strength, Deacon R wanted me to go and preach in that neighborhood. So I decided to preach one afternoon in their schoolhouse. When I arrived I found the place full. Deacon R was sitting near a window. They sang as best they could. I then prayed, and felt like I had real access into God's throneroom. I stood up and read this Scripture: "You serpents, you generation of vipers, how can you escape the damnation of hell?"

Deacon R looked very uneasy, and he soon got up and went and stood in the open door. I assumed that he had gone to keep some of the boys near the doorway still. But I later learned that it was because of fear. He thought that if they attacked me, he would be able to escape. He could see that I was going to be very direct with them; and he wanted to keep out of their reach. During that sermon I poured myself out upon them with all my might, and before I was through there was a complete overturning of the very foundations of Universalism in that place. It was very similar to what happened in Sodom. Thus the revival swept through every part of town, and some of the neighboring towns also.

During this revival there were two cases of instant recovery from insanity. As I went into a meeting one time, I saw several ladies sitting in a pew with a woman dressed in black who seemed to be in great distress. They were partly holding her and preventing her from getting out. One of the ladies came and told me that she was an insane woman – that she had been a Methodist but believed she had fallen from grace. This led to despair, and finally to insanity.

Her husband was a heavy drinker who lived several miles from the village. He had left her at the meeting and gone off to the tavern. I said a few words to her, but she replied that she had to go. She said she could not bear to hear praying, preaching or singing, because hell was her home and she could not endure anything that made her think of heaven.

I told the ladies to keep her in her seat if they could, without disturbing the meeting. I then went into the pulpit. As soon as the singing began she struggled hard to get out. But the ladies obstructed her, and kindly but persistently prevented her escape. After a few moments she became quiet, but seemed to be avoiding listening to the singing. I then prayed. For some time I heard her struggling to get out, but before I had finished she became quiet, and the congregation was still. The Lord gave me a great spirit of prayer, and a text from Hebrews: "Let us come boldly unto the throne of grace, that we may obtain mercy and find grace to help in time of need."

My aim was to encourage faith, in ourselves and in her. She kept her head down, and seemed determined not to listen to anything I said. But as I continued she gradually began to raise her head, and to look at me from inside her long black bonnet. She looked up more and more until she sat upright, and looked me in the face with intense concentration. As I urged the people to be bold in their faith, to launch out and commit themselves with total confidence to God through the sacrifice of our great High Priest, she suddenly startled the congregation with a loud shriek. She then threw herself almost out of her seat, and I could see that she was trembling. The ladies in the pew partly supported her, and watched her with prayerful interest and sympathy. As I went on she began to look up again, and soon sat upright, her face wonderfully changed, full of triumphant joy and peace. I have seldom seen a human face as radiant as hers that day. Her joy was so great that she could hardly contain herself until the meeting was over – and then she let everybody know that she had been set free. About two years later I met her again and she was still full of joy and peace.

The other case of recovery was that of a woman who had also fallen into despair and insanity. I was not there when she was restored, but I was told that it was almost instantaneous – and it occurred when she was baptized in the Holy Spirit. Revivals are sometimes accused of making people mad. But the fact is, people are naturally mad on the subject of religion, and revivals restore them rather than making them mad.

During this revival we heard that there was a lot of opposition to it from Gouverneur, a town about twelve miles further north. We heard that they threatened to come down and attack us and break up our meetings. Of course, we paid no attention. In fact, it wasn't long before revival hit that place as well.

Chapter Nine

REVIVALS THROUGHOUT THE REGION

People were begging me to stay at Evans' Mills, and I finally agreed that I would stay with them for at least a year. I had become engaged to a young lady, and we were married in Whitestown in October, 1824. A day or two after our wedding I returned to Evans' Mills to arrange for our furniture to be transported there. I told her she could expect me back in about a week.

The previous fall, I had preached a few times at a place called Perch River, northwest of Evans' Mills. I was intending to return for my wife about the middle of the week, but a messenger from Perch River came and said there had been a revival working its way slowly among the people ever since I preached there, and he begged me to go down and preach at least once more. I finally went down there on the Tuesday night, but I found the interest so deep that I stayed and preached on the Wednesday and Thursday nights as well. Finally I gave up on the idea of returning for my wife that week, and continued to preach in the neighborhood.

The revival soon spread in the direction of Brownville, a large village several miles to the southwest. At the urging of the church there, I went to Brownville for the winter, having written to my wife that due to the circumstances I would have to delay coming to get her until God opened the way.

God was moving in Brownville but the church was in such a state that it was difficult to get them involved. The behaviour of the leadership was a real hindrance to the revival at times. It was very frustrating, and there were a lot of obstacles to overcome. Sometimes I would find that the pastor and his wife had stayed away from the meetings to attend a party somewhere in town.

I was staying with an elder of the church who was one of the pastor's closest friends. One day I met him in the hall and he said to me, "Mr. Finney, what would you think of a man who was praying week after week for the Holy Spirit, with no result?" I replied that I would think he was praying from false motives. "But what are the right motives?" he asked. "If he wants to be happy, is that a false motive?" I replied, "Satan could well pray with as good a motive as that." I then quoted the words of the Psalmist: "Then will I teach transgressors your ways, and sinners will be converted." I pointed out: "The Psalmist did not pray for the Holy Spirit so he could be happy, but so he could be useful, and that sinners might be converted to Christ." After saying this I went out and he returned to his room.

I stayed out until dinner time and when I returned he said he had a confession to make: "Mr. Finney, I owe you an apology. I was angry when you said that to me, and I must confess that I hoped I would never see you again. What you said convicted me that I had never been truly converted, and that I had never had any higher motive than a mere selfish desire for my own happiness. After you left the house I prayed for God to take my life. I could not stand for people to know that I had been so deceived. I have been a close friend of the pastor, yet I saw that I had always been a deceived hypocrite. I couldn't stand it and I just wanted to die." However, he was truly broken before God, and from that time on he became a new man.

Early in the spring of 1825 I left Brownville with my horse and buggy, to go and pick up my wife. I had been absent for six months since our marriage, and because of the mail we had seldom been able to exchange letters. I drove about fifteen miles, but the roads were very slippery. I discovered that my horse needed new horseshoes. I stopped at Le Rayville, a small village about three miles south of Evans' Mills. While my horse was being shod, the people discovered I was there and insisted that I should preach at one o'clock in the schoolhouse.

I agreed, and when one o'clock came the place was packed. While I preached the Spirit of God came down with great power. The outpouring was so powerful that I agreed to spend the night there, and preach again in the evening. But the anointing increased more and more, so that in the evening I announced there would be another meeting in the morning, and in the morning I announced there would be another one in the evening. Soon I could see that I would not be able to make it to pick up my wife. I asked one of the men there if he could take my horse and buggy and pick her up for me. He did so, and I went on preaching from day to day and from night to night – and there was a powerful revival.

While I was in Brownville, God showed me in a totally unexpected way that he was going to pour out His Spirit in Gouverneur, and that I must go there and preach. I knew absolutely nothing about the place, except that there had been so much opposition to the revival in Antwerp there the year before. I have no idea how or why the Spirit of God made this clear to me. But it seems it was a direct revelation from God. In prayer I was shown, as clear as day, that I must go and preach in Gouverneur, and that God would pour out His Spirit there.

Soon afterwards I met one of the members of a church in Gouverneur, who was passing through Brownville. I told him what God had revealed to me. He stared at me as though I was mad. But I urged him to go home and tell the Christian people there what I had told him – so they could prepare for the outpouring of the Holy Spirit. He told me that there were two churches in Gouverneur standing near each other – and that the Baptists had a pastor but the Presbyterians had none.

Later, when revival broke out in Gouverneur and attracted a lot of attention, the Baptists began to oppose it. They spoke against it and tried to stop it in any way they could. This encouraged a group of young men to band together specifically to oppose the revival. The Baptist church was quite influential and the stand they took greatly aggravated the situation, and gave it a very bitter edge. These young men seemed to be standing right in the way of the revival.

Brother Nash and I made up our minds that this blockage must be overcome through prayer. Nothing else would do. We decided to pray until we prevailed with God – until He assured us that no power in hell or earth could stop the revival.

I did the preaching and Brother Nash gave himself almost continually to prayer. The next Sunday we met at five o'clock in the church for a prayer meeting. The place was full. Near the end of the meeting Brother Nash stood up and spoke to the group of young men who had banded together to oppose the revival. I think they were all there, and they sat bracing themselves up against the Spirit of God. It was too serious for them to really mock what they were hearing, yet everyone could see how stiff-necked they had become.

Brother Nash spoke to them in a very urgent way and pointed out the guilt and danger of the course they were taking. Near the end he became very fired-up and said to them, "Mark my words, young men! God will break your ranks in less than one week, either by converting some of you or by sending some of you to hell. He will do this as surely as the Lord is my God!" He brought his hand down on the top of the pew in front of him with jarring force. He sat down immediately, dropped his head and groaned with pain.

The house was as still as death, and most of the people had their heads down. I could see that the young men were very stirred up. From my point of view, I regretted that Brother Nash had gone so far. He had committed himself, that God would either take the life of some of them and send them to hell, or convert some of them within a week. However, on Tuesday morning the leader of these young men came to me in the great distress. He was desperate to submit to God, and as soon as I began to question him he broke down like a child, confessed, and gave himself to Christ. Then he asked, "What shall I do, Mr. Finney?" I replied "Go to all your friends and pray with them, and urge them to turn to the Lord." He did so and before the week was out, nearly all of those young men were converted.

Chapter Ten

REVIVALS IN DE KALB AND WESTERN

From Gouverneur I went to De Kalb, another village still further north. A few years before, there had been a revival there under the Methodists. There had been quite a lot of excitement, and many instances of what the Methodists call "falling under the power of God." The Presbyterians had opposed this and so there was quite a bit of bad feeling between the Methodists and the Presbyterians. As far as I could see it was the Presbyterians who had been in the wrong.

I had not preached long one evening when, just at the close of my sermon, I saw a man fall from his seat near the door, and the people gathered around to take care of him. It looked as if he had "fallen under the power of God", and I assumed he was a Methodist. I have to say, I was a little concerned that it might re-open old wounds. But I was surprised to find that it was one of the most influential members of the Presbyterian church who had fallen. And it was remarkable that during this revival, there were several cases of this happening among the Presbyterians, but none among the Methodists. This led to confessions and explanations amongst the members of both churches – until the friendship and good feeling between them was restored.

One afternoon there were some arrivals from Ogdensburgh and among them was Elder S. He went to the meeting in the morning, and was invited by Elder B to go home with him for lunch. Elder B was full of the Holy Spirit and on the way home he preached to Elder S, who had become very cold and backslidden in his walk with God. Elder S was deeply affected by his words.

As they sat down to lunch, Elder S asked Elder B, "How did you get this blessing?" Elder B replied, "I stopped lying to God. All my Christian life I have been full of pretense – asking God for things that I did not really want. I copied other people's prayers – often without meaning them at all – and basically lied to God. But as soon as I made up my mind that I would never say anything to God that I did not really mean, He answered me and filled me to overflowing with His Holy Spirit."

At that moment another visitor, who had not yet begun to eat, shoved his chair back from the table, and fell on his knees and began to confess how he had lied to God and how he had been a hypocrite in his prayers, as well as in his life. The Holy Spirit fell upon him immediately, and filled him as full as he could hold.

The next day Elder S returned to Ogdensburgh. But I understand he made many calls on the way, and prayed with many families. And thus the revival spread to Ogdensburgh.

In early October, the church synod that I belonged to met in Utica. I took my wife, and we went down to Utica to attend, and to visit her father's family who lived nearby.

Mr. Gale, my theological teacher, had left Adams not long after me, and had moved to a farm in Western Oneida County. We had not gone very far on our return journey when we met Mr. Gale in his carriage. He leaped out and said, "God bless you, Brother Finney! I was going down to the synod to see you. You must come home with me. I do not believe that I was ever converted." He was so insistent that I agreed, and we drove immediately to Western.

As I have stated before, the spirit of prayer that prevailed in all of these revivals was a very noticeable feature. It was common for young converts to be deeply burdened in prayer. Sometimes they felt compelled to pray all night until they were totally exhausted. The influence of the Holy Spirit was so strong on the minds of Christians that they seemed to carry the weight of immortal souls with them everywhere they went. They became extremely serious and watchful in what they said and did. Instead of chatting, when they met together it became common for them to fall on their knees in prayer.

Not only were there a lot more prayer meetings, but they were fully attended and they were often very serious and solemn. There was a lot of private prayer also. Many Christians spent hours in prayer. Sometimes two or more would take the promise, "If two of you agree on anything they shall ask, it shall be done for them by my Father in heaven," and make one particular person a focus of prayer. The answers came so often and so quickly that no-one could escape the conviction that God was daily and hourly answering prayer.

If anything happened that threatened to harm the work – if any root of bitterness, fanaticism or disorder sprang up – then the Christians would give themselves to prayer for God to direct and control things, and it was amazing how readily He was able to move the obstacles out of the way.

In my own experience, I have to say that unless I had the spirit of prayer I could do nothing. Even for a day or an hour – if I lost the spirit of grace and supplication, I found myself unable to preach with power and effectiveness, or to win souls by personal conversation. It has always been the same with me.

For several weeks before I left De Kalb to go to the synod, I was deeply burdened in prayer and had an experience that was quite new to me. I found myself so burdened down with the weight of immortal souls, that I was forced to pray without ceasing. Some of my experiences alarmed me. I would actually find myself saying to God that He had made a promise to answer prayer, and I could not and would not be denied. I felt so certain that He would hear me, and that faithfulness to His promises made it impossible that He would not hear and answer, that I found myself saying to Him, "I hope you do not think that I can be denied. I come with your faithful promises in my hand, and I cannot be denied." I cannot tell you how absurd unbelief looked to me, and how certain it was in my mind, that God would answer these prayers that I found myself praying in such agony and faith. I had no idea of the exact form the answer would take. But my impression was that the answer was near, even at the door, and I felt myself greatly strengthened in spirit. I put on the harness for a mighty conflict with the powers of darkness, and expected to see a far more powerful outpouring of the Spirit of God in that new country where I had been ministering.

I have spoken of my detour to Western as I was returning from the synod meeting. It was here that the 'Western revivals' began – which created quite a stir and were opposed by certain prominent ministers in the East, who raised the cry of "New Measures."

When we got to Western, Mr. Gale invited me to the prayer meeting that afternoon. They asked me to lead the meeting but I declined, preferring to hear them pray and talk rather than taking part myself. The meeting was opened by one of the elders. He made a long prayer, or perhaps I should say a narrative – I hardly know what to call it. He told the Lord how many years they had been holding that prayer meeting each week, and that no answer had ever come. He made a number of statements that greatly shocked me. After he had finished, another elder took up the same theme. In another long prayer he went over almost the same ground, covering anything that the first one had left out. Then the third elder did the same. By this time I could say, like Paul, that my spirit was stirred within me. They had finished and were about to close the meeting, when one of the elders asked me if I would say a few words. I stood up and, using their own statements and confessions, gave them an extremely searching talk.

When I stood up I had no idea what I would say, but the Spirit of God came upon me, and I took up their prayers and statements and confessions, and dissected them. I asked if they understood that their prayer meeting was a mock prayer meeting. Had they come together to mock God, by implying that all the blame for what had happened was His alone?

At first they looked angry. Some of them said later that they were on the point of getting up and leaving. But I followed them up on the track of their prayers and confessions, until the leading elder burst into tears and exclaimed, "Brother Finney, it's all true!" He fell to his knees and wept aloud. This was the signal for a general breaking. Every man and woman went down on their knees. There were probably only a dozen present, but they were the leading members of the church. They all wept and confessed, and broke their hearts before God. This scene continued for an hour, and a more thorough breaking and confession I have seldom seen.

As soon as they recovered a little, they begged me to stay and preach to them on the Sunday. I regarded it as the voice of the Lord, and agreed to do so. This was Thursday night. On Friday my mind was deeply burdened. I went into the church often to pray and found that I had a mighty hold on God. The news got around, and on Sunday the church was full. I preached all day, and God came down with great power upon the people. It was obvious to everyone that a move of God had begun. I made arrangements to preach in different parts of town, in the schoolhouses and so-on, and the revival increased on a daily basis.

In the meantime, I was deeply burdened in prayer. I also found that there was a real spirit of prayer, especially among the female members of the church. The wives of two of the elders of the church were greatly burdened in prayer.

I called in at Mr. H's and found him pale and anxious. He said to me, "Brother Finney, I think my wife will die. She is so burdened that she cannot rest day or night, but is totally given up to prayer. She has been in her room all morning groaning and struggling in prayer, and I am afraid it will completely overcome her strength." Hearing my voice she came out, and there was a heavenly glow on her face. She was radiant with a hope and a joy direct from heaven. She said, "Brother Finney, the Lord has come! This work will spread over all this region!" Her husband looked surprised and did not know what to say. It was new to him, but not to me. I had seen this kind of thing before, and I believed that prayer had indeed prevailed.

The revival continued to spread and strengthen, until it began to show clear signs of the direction in which the Spirit of God was leading from that place. It became clear that the revival was spreading in the direction of Rome and Utica.

I had preached and prayed almost continually during the time I had been at Mr. Gale's. I liked to pray out loud when I was alone, so I spread a buffalo robe in the hayloft to muffle the noise and spent a great deal of time there in secret prayer to God. Mr. Gale had told me several times that if I wasn't careful my health would break down. However, the Spirit of prayer was on me and I could not resist Him, but poured out my soul to God continually. It was November and the weather was becoming cold. Mr. Gale and I came home late one day but instead of going into the house, I crept up into the hayloft to pour out my burdened song to God in prayer. I prayed until the burden left me. I was so exhausted that I fell asleep almost instantly. The first I knew, Mr. Gale was climbing up into the hayloft saying, "Brother Finney, are you dead?" I awoke, not realizing where I was at first. But one thing I knew – that my mind was calm and my faith unwavering. The work would go on – I felt assured of that.

Chapter Eleven

REVIVALS IN NEW YORK STATE

I made my way to Rome, New York, and preached there three times one Sunday. It was clear to me that the Word had a powerful impact. I could see that many people were bowed down with deep conviction of sin. In the morning I preached from the Scripture, "The carnal mind is at enmity with God," and followed it up with something similar in the afternoon and evening. I waited until the pastor, Mr. Gillett returned, and told him what had happened. He didn't seem to realize that the work was beginning with such power. But he wanted to hold a "meeting for inquirers" anyway. As I have said before, the methods that I had used in promoting revivals were pretty simple: A lot of public and private prayer, preaching, personal conversation and visiting from house to house. And when there were people wanting to become Christians we held "inquirers meetings" for them. These were the only methods I had used up to that time.

Mr. Gillett asked me if I could be at the meeting of inquiry. I told him I would, if we could hold it on the Monday evening. It was to be at the home of one of his deacons. When we arrived we found the large sitting room full to overflowing. Mr. Gillett looked around with surprise, because many of the most intelligent and influential members of his congregation were there. We spent a brief time trying to talk with them, but I soon saw that emotions were running so high that there was danger of an outburst that would be almost uncontrollable. I said to Mr. Gillett, "We can't continue the meeting like this. I will say a few words, and then dismiss them."

Nothing had been said or done to create any excitement in the meeting. The emotion was totally spontaneous. The Spirit was moving with such power that even a few words of conversation would make the stoutest men writhe in their seats, as if a sword had been thrust into their hearts. I don't think it's possible for someone who has never witnessed such a scene, to realize what the force of the truth is sometimes like, under the power of the Holy Spirit. It was indeed a sword – a two-edged sword. The pain that it produced when a few searching words were spoken seemed unbearable.

Mr. Gillett became very agitated. He turned pale, and said to me, "What shall we do? What shall we do?" I put my hand on his shoulder and whispered, "Keep quiet, keep quiet, Brother Gillett." I then spoke to them as gently and plainly as I could about their only remedy. I pointed them to Christ as the Savior of the world, and kept on talking for as long as they could bear it, which was only a few moments.

Mr. Gillett became so agitated that I stepped up to him, took him by the arm and said, "Let us pray." We knelt down in the middle of the room. I prayed in a low, unemotional voice, interceding with the Savior that they might accept the salvation He offered and place their trust in Him. The emotion deepened every moment, and I could hear their sobs and sighs. I closed my prayer and stood up quickly. Everyone stood and I said, "Now please go home without speaking a word to each other. Try to keep silent, and go to your rooms."

At this moment a young man almost fainted and fell on some other young men standing near him – and they all partially fainted and fell down together. This produced a loud shrieking, but I hushed them up, and said to the young men, "Please open the door wide so everyone can go out in silence." They did as I asked. There was no more shrieking, but they went out sobbing and sighing. In fact, their sobs and sighs could be heard until they got out into the street.

The next morning, as soon as it was light, people began to call at Mr. Gillett's to have us go and visit members of their families whom they said were under great conviction. We ate a hasty breakfast and started out. As soon as we were in the streets, the people ran out and begged us to go into their homes. And whenever we went into a house the neighbors would rush in and fill the largest room. We would stay and talk for awhile and then go to another house – and the people would follow us around.

The state of things in that town was amazing. Convictions were so deep and universal that we would sometimes go into a house and find people either kneeling or face-down on the floor. We visited from house to house like this until midday. But I said to Mr. Gillett, "We can't go on this way. We need to hold a special meeting." He agreed, and went to the public schools to announce that at one o'clock there would be a special meeting. We went home, had our lunch, and started for the meeting. We saw people hurrying, and some even running to get there. They came from every direction. By the time we arrived, the large room was totally crammed with people. Men, women, and children crowded in.

This meeting was very similar to the one we'd had the night before. The emotion was overwhelming. Strong men were so cut down by the things that were said that they were unable to help themselves, and had to be taken home by their friends. The meeting went on until it was almost night. It resulted in a huge number of conversions, and the revival spread in every direction.

The atmosphere in the village – and the whole neighborhood – was such that nobody could even visit without feeling awed by the impression that God was there in an unusual and powerful way. One incident was particularly memorable. The sheriff of the county was based in Utica, but there was another courthouse as well – which was in Rome. So the sheriff had to come to Rome regularly on business. He later told me that he had heard what was happening there, and he and others had been laughing about it at the hotel where he boarded.

But one day it was necessary for him to come to Rome. He said he was glad because he wanted to see for himself what everyone was talking about. He drove in without feeling anything unusual at all, until he crossed over the old canal about a mile from town. He said as soon as he crossed the canal, a strange feeling came over him, an awe so deep that he could not shake it off. He felt as if God pervaded the whole atmosphere. This feeling increased the whole way, until he came to the village. He stopped at the hotel and the owner looked as if he felt just the same way – as if he was afraid to speak. Several times during his brief visit he had to get up from the table and go to the window to try and distract himself to keep from weeping. He could see that everybody seemed affected the same way. Such an awe, such a solemnity – like nothing he had never come across before. He hurriedly completed his business and returned to Utica. But he never spoke lightly of the revival in Rome again. And a few weeks later he was converted.

It is difficult to describe such a deep and widespread state of spiritual emotion, with no disorder or fanaticism, as we saw in Rome. Many of the converts of that revival are scattered all over America, and they will tell you that in those meetings there was great order and solemnity, and a lot of care was taken to guard against anything getting in that was not of God.

The Spirit's work was so spontaneous, so powerful and so overwhelming that we had to use great caution and wisdom in conducting the meetings, to prevent an outburst of emotion that would have quickly exhausted the people and brought about a reaction. But no reaction came. A sunrise prayer meeting was started, and I believe for more than a year it was very well attended. The morals of the people were so changed that Mr. Gillett often said it didn't seem like the same place. Any sin that was left had to hide its head. No open immorality could be tolerated. I have given only a very faint outline of what happened in Rome. A true description of all the moving incidents that were crowded into that revival could make a volume in itself.

I should say a few words about the spirit of prayer in Rome at that time. Wherever you went, you heard the voice of prayer. Walk along the street, and if two or three Christians happened to be together, they were praying. Wherever they met, they prayed.

Wherever there was a sinner unconverted, especially if he opposed the revival, you would find two or three brothers or sisters agreeing to make him a specific focus of prayer.

When I had been in Rome for about twenty days, one of the elders in Utica died, and I went down to attend his funeral. Mr. Aiken conducted the funeral and I learned from him that the spirit of prayer was already present in his congregation. He told me that one woman had been so deeply burdened about the state of the church and the unsaved in that city, that she had prayed for two days and nights almost continuously, until she could pray no more. She had such travail of soul that even when she was exhausted, she could not endure the burden she was under unless someone else could pray in her place – and express her desires to God.

I told Mr. Aiken that revival had already begun in her heart. He recognized it too, of course, and invited me to come and begin ministering amongst his people right away. I soon did so, and the work began at once. The Word had an immediate impact, and the place became filled with the presence of the Holy Spirit. Our meetings were crowded every night and the revival continued with great power, especially in the two Presbyterian congregations.

In the middle of this revival, a striking incident occurred. The Oneida presbytery met in Utica while the revival was at its height. An old minister who was a stranger to me was quite annoyed by the heat and fervor of the revival. He found that everyone was talking about it, and people were praying everywhere, even in the stores and other public places. He had never seen a revival before. He was a Scotsman and, I believe, had not been in the country very long.

During the presbytery meeting he made a violent speech against the revival. What he said shocked and grieved many of the Christians who were there. They felt like falling on their faces before God, and crying out to Him to prevent what was said from doing any harm.

The presbytery adjourned for the evening. Some of the members went home, and others remained overnight. Christians gave themselves to prayer. There was a great crying out to God that night, that He would turn back any evil influence resulting from that speech. The next morning, the old minister was found dead in his bed.

During these revivals, people from distant towns heard what God was doing, and came to see for themselves. Many of them were converted to Christ.

Another incident occurred in this same region. There was a cotton factory just above Whitesboro, now called New York Mills. It was owned by a non-Christian – but a good man. I preached nearby in the village schoolhouse one evening, which was large and crowded with hearers. I could see that the Word made a powerful impact on the people, especially the young people who worked in the factory.

The next morning I visited the factory to have a look. As I went through, I noticed that those who were busy at their looms and other machines seemed agitated. Walking through one part where there were many young women working, I saw a couple of them looking at me and speaking very seriously to each other. They seemed agitated, although they both laughed. I walked slowly towards them. One of them was trying to mend a broken thread, and I saw that her hands trembled so much that she couldn't fix it. The girl grew more and more distressed, and could not continue. When I came within eight or ten feet of her, I looked solemnly at her. She sank down and burst into tears. This caught on almost like gunpowder, and in a moment nearly everybody in the room was in tears. This spread through the factory. The owner was there, and seeing the state of things he said to the foreman, "Stop the mill and let the people attend to religion. It is more important that our souls be saved than that this factory run." The factory was shut down and I scarcely ever saw a more powerful meeting than that one. It was a huge building and many people worked there. The revival went through the mill with incredible power, and in a few days nearly everybody there was converted.

Dr. Lansing, pastor of the First Presbyterian Church in Auburn, came to Utica to see the revival there. He urged me to go and minister for a time with him and I agreed. But when I arrived in Auburn in 1826, I found that some of the professors in the theological seminary there were taking a hostile attitude to the revival.

I had been aware that a large number of ministers east of Utica were writing letters about the revivals, and taking a hostile stand against them. But until I came to Auburn I was not fully aware of the amount of opposition I was destined to meet from these ministers – who did not personally know me but were influenced by false reports. Soon after I arrived in Auburn I learned that a secret network was developing with the aim of uniting the ministers and churches to hedge me in, and prevent the revivals from spreading.

I was told that all the New England churches in particular were closed to me. I became quite upset by all of this. I didn't say anything to anyone, but gave myself to prayer. I asked God to direct me and to give me the grace to ride out the storm.

One day I was in my room and the Lord showed me a vision of what lay ahead. He drew so near to me while I was praying that I literally trembled. I shook from head to foot, under a full sense of the presence of God. It seemed more like being on the top of Sinai, with all the thunderings, than in the presence of the cross of Christ.

Never in my life was I so awed and humbled before God. But instead of wanting to run away, I felt drawn nearer and nearer to this Presence that filled me with such awe and trembling. After a period of great brokenness before Him, there came a great lifting up. God assured me that He would be with me and hold me up – that no opposition would succeed against me. He showed me that there was nothing I should do, but to keep ministering and allow

Him to vindicate my ministry.

The sense of God's presence, and all that passed between myself and God at that time, I can never describe. It led me to be perfectly trusting, perfectly calm, and to have nothing but the best attitude towards all the brothers who were misled and were aligning themselves against me. I felt sure that everything would turn out alright in the end – that the best course for me to take was to leave everything to God and just keep on going. As the storm gathered and the opposition increased, I never doubted for one moment how it would result. I was never disturbed by it. I never spent a waking hour thinking about it – even when it seemed as if all the churches in the land, except where I had ministered, would unite to shut me out of their pulpits. This was what the leaders of this opposition had vowed to do. They were so deceived that they thought they had no choice but to unite and, as they expressed it, "put him down." But God assured me that they would never put me down.

Soon after my arrival in Auburn, an interesting incident occurred. My wife and I were the guests of Dr. Lansing, the pastor of the church. His congregation was quite worldly in a lot of ways, and non-Christians accused them of being leaders in fashion and worldliness. As usual my preaching was aimed at the reformation of the church – to get them into a revival state. One Sunday I preached as searchingly as I could on this issue of worldliness. The Word took a deep hold on the people.

At the end of my sermon I asked the pastor to pray. He agreed strongly with my sermon, and before he prayed he spoke to the church, confirming what I had said to them. Suddenly a man stood up in the gallery and said, "Mr. Lansing, I do not believe that such talk from you can do any good while you wear a ruffled shirt and a gold ring, and while your wife and members of your family sit there, dressed as leaders in the fashions of the day." It seemed like this would kill Dr. Lansing outright. He made no reply, but threw himself across the side of the pulpit and wept like a child. The congregation was almost as shocked and affected as he was. They almost all dropped their heads and many of them wept openly.

Apart from the sobs and sighs, the house was deathly silent. I waited a few moments, but Dr. Lansing did not move, so I said a brief prayer and dismissed the congregation.

I went home with the dear, wounded pastor. He took the ring off his finger – it was a slender gold ring that could hardly attract attention – and said that his first wife, on her death bed, had taken it off her finger and placed it on his, asking that he wear it for her sake. He had done so, without a thought of it being a stumbling-block. He said he had worn ruffles since his childhood, and thought nothing of them. "But if these things are a stumbling-block to others," he said, "I will not wear them." He was a good man and an excellent pastor.

Soon after this, the church decided to make a public confession to the world of their backsliding and their unchristian attitudes. A confession was written, covering everything. It was submitted to the church for their approval, and then read in front of the congregation. The church stood, many of them weeping, while the confession was read. From that time the revival went on with greatly increased power.

Chapter Twelve

REVIVAL AT OBERLIN COLLEGE

In January 1835, Rev. John Shipherd and Rev. Asa Mahan persuaded me to go to Oberlin College, Ohio, as professor of theology. So I ended up spending my summers in Oberlin and my winters in New York for several years. Students thronged to the College from every direction.

Businessman Arthur Tappan had promised to finance the College until we no longer needed his help. But we had only just started putting up the buildings, and still needed a large amount of money, when a great financial crash decimated Mr. Tappan's business, and nearly all of the men who had agreed to support the faculty.

For years afterwards we struggled with poverty. At one stage, I saw no way of providing for my family through the winter. Thanksgiving Day arrived and found us so poor that I had to sell my travelling trunk which I had used in my evangelistic ministry, to replace a cow which I had lost. I woke up on Thanksgiving morning and placed our needs before the Lord in prayer. I said that if help did not come I would assume that it was for the best, and that I would be completely satisfied with whatever God wanted to do. I went and preached, and enjoyed my own preaching as well as I ever did. I had a blessed day, and I could see that the people truly enjoyed it as well.

After the meeting my wife returned home. When I reached the gate, she was standing in the open door with a letter in her hand. She said, "The answer has come, my dear," and handed me a letter containing a check from Mr. Josiah Chapin of Providence for two hundred dollars. He had been here the previous summer with his wife. I had said nothing about our needs at all, as I had never been in the habit of mentioning them to anybody. In the letter he said that I could expect more from time to time. He continued to send me six hundred dollars a year for several years, and on this we managed to live.

We had a wonderful revival whenever I returned to New York. We also had a revival in Oberlin continually. Very few students came without being converted.

I am convinced that the higher realms of Christian spirituality can only be gained through a terribly searching application of God's Law to the human conscience and heart.

Over a period of time I became very dissatisfied with my own lack of stability in faith and love. God did not allow me to backslide to the same degree as some other Christians. But I often felt weak when the devil tempted me, and I often needed to hold days of fasting and prayer, and to spend time overhauling my own spiritual life, in order to keep the close communion with God that I needed for revival ministry.

In looking at the state of the church I had to wonder whether there wasn't something higher and more enduring than the church was aware of – whether there was a higher form of Christian life. I was aware of the 'Sanctification' that the Methodists taught. I spent hours searching the Scriptures and reading whatever came to hand on the subject until I became convinced that there really is a higher and more stable form of Christian life – and it is available to every Christian.

This led me to preach two sermons on 'Christian Perfection', where I aimed to prove that it really is attainable in this life. I was convinced that the doctrine of "entire sanctification" (the ability of Christians to live without known sin) was a doctrine taught in the Bible, and that God had already made available to us a way to live in this state.

The last winter that I spent in New York, the Lord brought a great refreshing upon me. After a time of brokenness and soul-searching, He brought me into a large place and poured a sweetness into my soul similar to that which Edwards says he experienced. That winter I went through a thorough breaking – to such a degree that sometimes I could not keep from weeping loudly over my own sins and also the love of God. Such times were frequent that winter, and resulted in a great renewal of my spiritual strength. They also added to my views of the depths of what God had provided for Christians, and the abundance of His grace.

I know my views on Sanctification have been the subject of a lot of criticism. After a year or two, the cry of 'antinomian perfectionism' was heard, and this charge was brought against us. Letters were written and ecclesiastical bodies were consulted, and a great effort was made to present our views as totally heretical. Throughout the land, many ecclesiastical bodies passed resolutions warning against the influence of Oberlin theology. There seemed to be a huge uniting of ministers against us. But we said nothing.

The policy that we have always held to, was to leave the opposition alone. We kept to our own business, and always had as many students as we knew what to do with. Our hands were full, and God always encouraged us in our work.

Nowdays it is hard for people to realize the opposition that we met with when we first established the college. But none of this opposition ruffled our spirits or made us want to fight back. During these years of smoke and dust, of misunderstanding and opposition from without, the Lord was blessing us richly within. Not only were we prospering in our own souls, but we had a continuous revival – we were in what could be called a 'revival state.' Our students were converted by the hundreds and the Lord overshadowed us continually with the cloud of His mercy. God's Spirit swept over us continually from year to year, producing the fruit of the Spirit in abundance – love, joy, peace, long-suffering, gentleness, goodness, faith, meekness, and self-control. I have always attributed our success entirely to the grace of God.

During the winter of 1843 the Lord gave me another thorough overhauling and a fresh baptism of His Spirit. My mind was greatly burdened on the question of personal holiness – and the church's lack of power and faith in God.

I gave myself to a great deal of prayer. I would go to bed as early as I could, rising at four o'clock in the morning because I could no longer sleep, and go to the study to pray. I was so deeply absorbed in prayer that I often continued from four o'clock until breakfast at eight o'clock. My days were spent searching the Scriptures. I read nothing else all that winter but my Bible, and a great deal of it seemed new to me. Again the Lord seemed to take me from Genesis to Revelation. He led me to see the connection of things – the promises, the threatenings, the prophecies and their fulfillment. The whole Scripture seemed ablaze with the light and the life of God.

Just before this, I had a great struggle to consecrate myself to God in a greater way than I had ever thought possible. I had often laid my family on the altar before God. But during this time I had a great struggle in giving up my wife to God's will. She was in very poor health, and it was evident that she could not live long. I had never seen so clearly what it meant to lay her and all that I possessed on the altar of God. For hours I struggled on my knees to give her up without reserve to the will of God. But I found myself unable to do it. I was so shocked and surprised at this that I was literally sweating with agony. I struggled and prayed until I was exhausted, and found myself unable to give her up.

But later I was enabled to fall back in a deeper sense than ever before, on the perfect will of God. I then told the Lord that I had such confidence in Him that I was totally willing to give myself, my wife and my family, all for Him to do with whatever He willed.

I understood consecration to God in a deeper way than ever before. I spent a long time on my knees pondering the whole thing, and giving up everything to the will of God – the interests of the church, the progress of Christianity, the conversion of the world, and even the salvation or damnation of my own soul. In fact I went so far as to say to the Lord, with all my heart, that He could do anything with me or mine that He wanted. I had such a confidence in His goodness and love that I believed He could do nothing to which I could object. I felt a kind of holy boldness in telling Him this. So deep and perfect a resting in the will of God I had never known before.

I gave up my hope, and rested everything on a new foundation. I remember telling the Lord that I did not know whether He intended to save me or not. I did not even feel concerned to know. I said that if I found that He was preparing me for heaven, working holiness and eternal life in my soul, I would assume that He intended to save me. But if, on the other hand, I found myself empty of His light and love, I would conclude that He saw it wise and expedient to send me to hell – and either way I would accept His will. My mind settled into a perfect stillness.

This was early in the morning, and through the whole of that day I seemed to be in a state of perfect rest, body and soul. The question often arose in my mind during the day, "Do you still abide in the will of God?" I said without hesitation, "Yes, I take nothing back. I have no reason to take anything back." The thought that I might be lost did not distress me. Indeed, during that whole day I could not find in my mind the least fear, the least disturbing emotion. Nothing troubled me. I was neither elated or depressed, I was neither joyful or sorrowful. My confidence in God was perfect and my mind was as calm as heaven.

In the evening the question arose in my mind, "What if God sends me to hell, what then?" – "I would not object to it." "But can He send a person to hell who accepts His will in the sense that you do?" This question was no sooner raised in my mind than settled. I said, "No, it is impossible. Hell could be no hell to me, if I accepted God's perfect will." This sprung a vein of joy in my mind that kept developing more and more for weeks and months, and indeed years. For years my mind was too full of joy to feel really anxious on any subject. My prayers seemed to all run into, "Your will be done." It seemed as if my desires were all met. What I had been praying for I had received in a way that I did not expect. "Holiness to the Lord" seemed to be inscribed on all my thoughts. I had such a strong faith that God would accomplish His perfect will, that I did not care about anything. When I went to God to commune with Him as I often did, I would fall on my knees and find it impossible to ask for anything except that His will might be done in earth as it is in heaven. My prayers were swallowed up in that, and I often found myself smiling, as it were, in the face of God, and saying that I did not want anything. I was very sure that He would accomplish all that He wanted to – and my soul was completely satisfied with that.

It seemed as if my soul was wedded to Christ in a way I had never even thought or imagined before. In fact the Lord lifted me so far above anything I had ever experienced, and taught me so much of the meaning of the Bible, that I often found myself saying to Him, "I had never imagined that such a thing was true." It seemed to me that the passage, "My grace is sufficient for you," meant so much that it was a wonder I had never understood it before. I found myself saying, "Wonderful! Wonderful! Wonderful!" as these revelations were made to me. I spent the remainder of the winter teaching the people about the fullness there is in Christ. But I found that I preached over the heads of the majority of them. Most did not understand me. There were some that did, and they were wonderfully blessed.

I had often experienced unspeakable joy and very deep communion with God, but all this had fallen into the shade under these new experiences. I would often tell the Lord that I had never had any concept of the wonderful things revealed in the Gospel, and the wonderful grace there is in Jesus Christ.

As the excitement of that period faded and my mind became more calm, I saw more clearly the different steps of my Christian walk, and came to recognize the connection of things that had been put in place by God from beginning to end. Since then I have felt a religious freedom, a buoyancy and delight in God and His Word, a steadiness of faith, an overflowing love and liberty, that I had only experienced occasionally before.

A few years after this time of refreshing, my darling wife died. This was a great sorrow to me. However, I did not feel any murmuring or resistance to the will of God. I gave her up to Him without any resistance whatever. But I was very sad. The night after she died I was lying in my room alone, and some Christian friends were sitting in the living room, watching through the night. I had been asleep for a little while, and as I awoke the thought of my bereavement flashed over my mind with such power! My wife was gone! I would never hear her speak again, or see her face! Her children were motherless! What should I do? My brain seemed to reel, as if my mind was going. I rose from my bed exclaiming, "I will go insane if I cannot rest in God." The Lord soon calmed my mind, but still at times waves of sorrow would come over me that were almost overwhelming.

One day I was on my knees, communing with God on the subject, when suddenly he seemed to say to me, "You loved your wife?" "Yes," I said. "Well, did you love her for her own sake, or for your sake? Did you love her or yourself? If you loved her for her own sake, why are you so sad that she is with Me? Shouldn't her happiness with Me make you rejoice instead of mourn, if you loved her for her own sake?"

I can never describe the feelings that came over me when I heard these words. My whole state of mind was changed instantaneously. From that moment, sorrow was gone forever. I no longer thought of my wife as dead, but alive, and in the midst of the glories of heaven. My faith was so strong and my mind so filled with the light of God, that it seemed as if I could enter into the same state of mind that she was in, in heaven. I felt like I experienced the same state of profound, unbroken rest in the perfect will of God. I could see that this is the essence of heaven, and I experienced it in my own soul. I have never to this day lost the blessing of this state of mind.

These are experiences in which I have lived a great deal since that time. But in preaching, I have found that there is nowhere that I can preach these truths and be understood, except by a very small number. I have found that very few appreciate these teachings on the fullness of Christ's salvation, upon which my own soul delights to feed. Everywhere I am forced to come down to where the people are in order to make them understand me, and I have found that most churches are in such a low state that they are utterly incapable of understanding what I regard as the most precious truths of the whole Gospel.

When preaching to unconverted sinners I am forced, of course, to go back to first principles. In my own experience I have so long passed these outposts and first principles that I cannot live on those truths. However, I have to preach them to the unsaved to see them converted. But it is only now and then that I find it really worthwhile to pour out to Christians the fullness that my own soul sees in Christ. Even here in Oberlin, the majority of believers do not understandingly embrace these truths. They do not oppose them, and as far as they understand them they are convinced. But as a matter of experience they are ignorant of the highest and most precious truths of the Gospel of salvation in Jesus Christ.

POSTSCRIPT – by Andrew Strom

There is no doubt in my mind that Charles Finney was the most dominant and influential figure in world Christianity during the nineteenth century. We have just been reading about the way God used him in his early Revivals, but he grew in stature and influence decade after decade, right through the middle part of the century. And in the Western nations it was a century of Revivals like no other.

In 1829 Finney conducted his first Revival meetings in a large city – Philadelphia. The pattern was always the same – fearless 'repentance' preaching (in the mold of John the Baptist), and 'agonizing' prayer. And there was often great opposition – especially from other ministers – many of whom had never heard him preach.

In 1830 he preached in New York City for the first time, and a Christian newspaper was founded called the 'New York Evangelist' to publicise his views on Revival. In 1831 he went to Rochester, New York, where he saw one of the most powerful Revivals of his life. In fact, it was so powerful that its infuence was felt right through the United States and an estimated 100,000 people were converted in the space of just one year.

In 1833 Finney became pastor of the Chatham Street Chapel in New York City – a church that would become a leader in the anti-slavery movement by refusing to admit slaveholders to communion.

In 1835 one of Finney's most influential books was published – his 'Revival Lectures'. Thousands of copies were sold and the book made its way around the world, where it sparked Revivals in many places – even after his death. It was basically a book on "How to see true Revival occur". 1835 was also the year that he accepted the position of Professor of Theology at Oberlin College, Ohio – a post that he held right up until his death. He spent several years dividing his time between the church in New York and the College in Ohio. Again, there was continual opposition to his ministry during these years. But there was also continual Revival.

Eventually Finney left the pastorate in New York and based himself out of Oberlin. He continued to hold Revival meetings in various towns and cities during the non-academic part of each year. In 1846 he published his well-known book on Systematic Theology, and in 1849-1850 he visited England on a preaching tour for the first time, where he saw God move powerfully.

I am convinced that Finney's Revival ministry helped to set the scene for the great Prayer Revival of 1857-1858, during which an estimated two million people were converted in the space of just two years. Speaking of this powerful awakening, Finney wrote: "For a time it was estimated that at least fifty thousand conversions were occurring per week. Daily prayer meetings were established right across the Northern states. I remember in one of our meetings in Boston, a gentleman got up and said, "I am from Omaha, Nebraska. On my journey east I have found a continuous prayer meeting all the way – a prayer meeting about two thousand miles long."

A short time later the Revival jumped the Atlantic into the United Kingdom. And it just so happened that Finney was due to minister in England and Scotland in 1859-1860, which coincided with the height of the Revival there. Perfect timing! One of the movements that was greatly impacted by Finney's ministry was the early Salvation Army, which was started by William Booth in England not long after the Revival. They modeled a lot of their preaching on Finney.

In 1868, Finney completed work on his autobiography, which was published after his death eight years later (this book is based on it). Even in his final months Finney was still preaching. He died in Oberlin on August 16, 1875 at the ripe old age of 82 – a Revivalist to the very end.

CPSIA information can be obtained
at www.ICGtesting.com
Printed in the USA
BVOW09s0525311017
499041BV00001B/89/P